Making Your Own Will

Making Your Own Will

A Self-Help Guide

2nd edition

GORDON BOWLEY

howtobooks

'Let's choose executors and talk of wills.'
Richard II, Act III, Scene II – William Shakespeare.

Published by How To Books Ltd,
3 Newtec Place, Magdalen Road,
Oxford OX4 1RE. United Kingdom.
Tel: (01865) 793806. Fax: (01865) 248780.
email: info@howtobooks.co.uk
http://www.howtobooks.co.uk

British Library Cataloguing in Publication Data
A catalogue record for this book is available from the British
Library

Produced for How To Books by Deer Park Productions,
Tavistock.
Typeset by PDQ Typesetting, Newcastle-under-Lyme, Staffs.
Cover design by Baseline Arts Ltd, Oxford.
Printed and bound by Cromwell Press, Trowbridge, Wiltshire.

NOTE: The material contained in this book is set out in good
faith for general guidance and no liability can be accepted
for loss or expense incurred as a result of relying in particular
circumstances on statements made in the book and the book is
bought and sold on that basis. The laws and regulations are
complex and liable to change, and readers should check the
current position with the relevant authorities before making
personal arrangements.

Contents

Note from the author   xiii

1 Why Should You Make a Will?   **1**

It is your money and you want to decide who shall have
it   1

Do you really have nothing to leave but your debts?   3

Are you too young and not ready to die?   4

If you have to go, you should go your way (or try to)   4

They are your children and you should decide who shall
bring them up   4

Hasn't the government taken enough tax from you in
your lifetime?   5

Sparing your next of kin extra pain   6

Some matters really are urgent   7

What happens if you die without a valid will (in greater
detail!)   7

Who will administer your estate?   7

Who will inherit your estate?   8

What will happen to your business?   14

2 Can You Make a Will and How to Do It   **15**

Can you make a will?   15

Formalities   17

Your will must be made in writing   18

Your will must be signed by you or by someone in your
presence and at your request   19

Your signature on the will must be made or
acknowledged by you in the presence of two or more
witnesses who must be present at the same time   20

Each witness must sign the will and either sign or
acknowledge his signature in your presence   20

It must be apparent that you intend to give effect to the
will by signing it   20

A few general words on the subject of signing the will
and witnesses   21

Conventions   22
   Format   23
Precautions against fraud   25

3 What Can be Left in Your Will?   **26**
General principles   26
Mutual wills   28
Jointly owned property, i.e. property not in your sole
   name   31
Business partnerships   33
Property you do not own   33
   Insurance policies taken out or held on trust for
   another   33
   Other property you do not own over which you have a
   power of appointment   34
   Other property you do not own over which you have no
   power of appointment   34
Nominated property   35
Property which by its nature has restricted alienability   36
   Some existing rights in relation to land   36
   Shares in some limited companies   36
Your body   36
Statutory restrictions on your right to leave your assets to
   whom you choose   37
   Statutory tenancies   37
   The Inheritance (Provision for Family and
   Dependants) Act 1975 as amended   38
Intangible assets   40
Private pension scheme benefits   41

4 Matters to be Considered When Contemplating
Making Your Will   **42**
Joint wills   42
The number of executors   42
Whom should you choose to be your executors?   43
The appointment of guardians for your children by will   46
Your funeral and the disposal of your body after your
   death   51
Factors to consider which might influence your choice
   of beneficiaries   55

Avoiding challenges to your will   55
Elderly beneficiaries   55
The matrimonial home   56
Gifts to the young and age-contingent gifts   58
Bequests to spendthrifts and bankrupts   61
*Bequests to those incapable of managing their affairs
or suffering from other disabilities*   63
Inheritance tax and saving tax in your will   65
Inheritance tax   65
*What you can do in your will to minimise inheritance
tax*   76
Lifetime gifts by the terminally ill   77
*Equalisation of estates between spouses, the surviving
spouse exemption and the nil rate band*   77
*The use of survivorship clauses and bequests to your
spouse*   82
Special rules where exempt beneficiaries are involved   84
   'Grossing up' of legacies and gifts   84
   'Related property' valuation rules   86
   Cohabitees and the surviving spouse exemption   87
Skipping a generation   87

**5 Clauses Recommended to be Included and Clauses
   Recommended to be Excluded from Your Will**   **88**
Your name and address   88
The date of the will   89
A revocation clause   89
The appointment of executors   89
Alternative provisions for bequests to beneficiaries who
predecease you and for bequests that fail   90
Clauses relating to the remarriage of your spouse or the
registration of your civil partner's new partnership after
your death and provision for children of your previous
marriage or registered partnership   93
Mirror/mutual wills   95
Survivorship clauses   95
Who bears the debts, funeral expenses and expenses
incurred in carrying out your will and inheritance tax?   96
Gifts of property which is mortgaged or subject to a
financial charge   96

Gifts for life   97
Additional administrative powers in wills   97
   Powers of maintenance and advancement in relation
   to contingent gifts and gifts to minors   98
   Powers of investment and borrowing   98
   Receipt clauses for bequests to minors and bequests
   to organisations   99
   Beneficiaries who cannot be found   99
   Limited interests and apportionment of income   100
   Power for executor to carry on a business   100
   Power for executor to buy property from your estate   100
   Power to appoint new trustees   101
   Beneficiaries' power to remove trustees   101
   The duty of trustees of land to consult with
   beneficiaries   101
   The extent of liability for acts done in the
   administration of your estate   102
   Attestation clause   102
   Settling old scores   103

**6 Points on Which You Should Take Special Care When
   Drafting Your Will   104**
Identification of beneficiaries   106
Description of bequests   108
Legacies to those who owe you money and to those to
whom you owe money   110
The meaning of some words and phrases   110
Void provisions in wills   112
   Gifts to those who witness your will   113
   Gifts which are contrary to law or public policy   113
   Gifts which infringe the rules against perpetuities and
   accumulations   115
Section 33 of the Wills Act 1837 (as amended)   115
The effect of Divorce or Annulment of your marriage
or Dissolution of civil partnership on your will   116
   Effect on bequests to your spouse or civil partner   116
   Effect on spouse's or partner's power of appointment,
   executorship and trusteeship   116
   Effect on your spouse or partner as guardian   116

7   **The International Element of Wills**   **118**
    Formalities for completion of a valid will if you are
    outside England and Wales   118
    Wills relating to property which is situated out of
    England and Wales   120

8   **Revoking or Amending Your Will**   **122**
    Amending your will   122
    Revoking your will   123
    The privileged wills of those engaged in actual
    military service and sailors at sea   123
    Revocation by marriage or civil partnership   123
    Revocation by destroying the will with the intention to
    revoke it   124
    Implied revocation   125
    Express revocation   125
    Dependent relative revocation   125

9   **General Advice Concerning Wills and Associated**
    Matters   **127**
    The safekeeping of your will   127
    Information for your executors   129
    Living wills and advance directives   131
    Enduring Powers of Attorney   134
    Periodic reviews, deeds of family arrangement and
    two-year discretionary trusts   140

Appendix: Specimen Forms and Documents   **145**
    Specimen form of notice of severance of joint tenancy   145
    Specimen note as to reasons why a potential claimant
    under the Inheritance (Provision for Family and
    Dependants) Act 1975 has been left no or only a
    limited inheritance   146
    Basic skeleton form of a will with the residuary
    beneficiaries to benefit equally   147
        Notes   149
    Alternative provision to be used in the skeleton form
    of a will if you wish to leave the estate to your spouse
    for life or until she remarries and afterwards to
    other beneficiaries   151

Notes   151
Alternative provision to be used in the skeleton form
of a will if you wish the residuary beneficiaries to benefit
unequally   153
   Notes   154
Will leaving the entire estate to spouse and appointing
her as the sole executrix with alternative provisions
should she die before the testator   155
   Notes   158
Additional clauses to be inserted in a will   160
   In a will made with a marriage in mind   160
   In a will containing gifts to under age beneficiaries 160
     Appointment of guardians   160
     Advancement clause   160
     Receipt clause for a bequest   161
     Power to invest and borrow   161
   In a will which contains a bequest to an organisation 161
     Receipt clause for a bequest   161
     Bequest and receipt clause for a bequest to a 161
     charity
   In a will which contains a gift for life or time-
contingent interest   162
     Power of investment   162
     Exclusion of the rules of apportionment   162
     Advancement clause   162
     Personal benefit by trustees   162
     Exclusion of statutory provisions relating to
     trustees duty to consult with beneficiaries and
     beneficiaries' power to appoint and remove trustees 162
   In the will of a testator who is involved in a business 163
Specimen form of codicil   163
Specimen attestation clauses for use in wills and
codicils in special situations   164
   Attestation clause for use in the will or codicil of
   a testator who cannot write but makes his mark   164
   Note   164
   Attestation clause for use in the will or codicil of
   a testator who cannot make a mark or write   165
   Note   165

*Attestation clause for use in the will or codicil of a
testator who is blind* 166
Note 166
Specimen form of living will 167
Note 168

**Checklist for use after you have prepared your will but
before you sign it** **169**

Glossary **175**

Index **179**

Note from the author

This book is written to assist you whether you wish to prepare your own will or to use a professional to make one for you. It follows a logical step-by-step approach and I hope that it will alert you to the many and broad-ranging matters to be considered when you take the important step and 'have your last say'. In the book I have tried to deal not only with the formal, factual, legal requirements and technicalities of making a will, but also to incorporate something of what I gained from the experience of making and proving thousands of wills in over thirty years practising as a family solicitor, and to set out some of the things a solicitor would tell you if you could afford to pay for the time it would take.

Throughout the book I have tried to use as few legal terms as conveniently possible and I have included a glossary to help you to understand those that have been used. I have also included an appendix that contains specimens of various forms referred to in the book and specimen wills and clauses and a checklist.

I hope that you will find the book useful.

Gordon Bowley

Important notice

This book only deals with the law applicable to England and Wales. Scottish law is different. Moreover, law and practice do change frequently and while every effort has been made to ensure that the contents of the book are accurate and up to date, no responsibility is accepted for any loss resulting from acting, or from failure to act, as a result of it and the book is sold and bought on that basis. In particular, changes which might be made to the inheritance tax nil rate exemption band or tax rates in future Finance Acts, should be borne in mind, especially when reading the calculations made in Chapter 4.

Throughout the book, 'he' should be read as 'she' or 'they' where the context and circumstances require.

Why Should You Make a Will?

IT IS YOUR MONEY AND YOU WANT TO DECIDE WHO SHALL HAVE IT

It is self-evident that after death you can no longer personally manage, control or direct the destination of the assets you have so painstakingly acquired during your life or who is to benefit from what remains of them. Neither is it possible for you to personally have any direct input in the upbringing of your children.

If on death, which comes to us all and sometimes when we least expect it, you leave a valid will, it is possible at least indirectly to influence such matters. If you leave no valid will you are said to die intestate and these matters are decided in the main by the state, which is what few would wish and which sometimes has disastrous consequences. By making a will you will have more control over these and other matters and the flexibility which a will gives will bring peace of mind as to what will happen after your death.

The laws of intestacy do not rank highly on the political agenda and were mostly enacted in 1925. Only occasional and piecemeal revisions have been made since that date. The result is that they are out of date and unsuitable for British society in the twenty-first century in which marriage to a lifetime partner is no longer the norm.

In brief, in the case of death without a valid will, who inherits and deals with the winding up of what you leave (known as your estate) depends upon the size of your estate and what relatives, if any, survive you, and these are both matters of chance. If no relatives within a prescribed degree survive you, the Crown or the Duchies of Lancaster or Cornwall will inherit and wind up your estate, which is something that most people would wish to avoid. Moreover, it is more likely that it will be possible to trace those entitled under your will than to trace perhaps long-lost relatives entitled under the laws of intestacy.

Other problems can arise if you do not leave a valid will:

◆ If the value of your matrimonial home is high in proportion to the total value of your estate and children or sometimes some other relatives survive you, your spouse might be compelled to sell the matrimonial home to pay out the children or relatives. Similarly if your spouse dies intestate, you might be compelled to sell your home or other assets to pay out the entitlement of in-laws who might be people you tolerate rather than like. If you or your spouse die intestate, you cannot rely upon your children, relatives or in-laws, who might have the kindest of intentions towards you, permitting your spouse or yourself (as the case may be) to remain in the matrimonial home; their hands may be forced by their matrimonial or business problems and they may have no alternative but to compel you to sell property and claim their share of the estate immediately.

- If your marriage has broken down but no decree absolute of annulment or divorce has been pronounced at the date of your death, then under the laws of intestacy or under a previous will which you may not have revoked, depending upon the circumstances of your particular case, your surviving spouse might inherit the whole or a share of your estate which is totally inconsistent with your wishes.

- If you are a person with a cohabitee (partner) with whom you have set up home and you die intestate, your partner has no automatic right to inherit anything from you unless your partnership has been registered under the Civil Partnership Act 2004 and to inherit must make a prompt application to, and rely upon the tender mercies of, a court.

DO YOU REALLY HAVE NOTHING TO LEAVE BUT YOUR DEBTS?

This may seem to be true at first sight, but not upon further reflection. In a financial sense, you are probably worth more when you are dead than when you are alive; for example, if you are negligently killed in an accident your estate might be entitled to a very large sum by way of damages. If you die within a few years of taking out a life or endowment policy, your estate or the beneficiaries of that policy would certainly receive more than you would have received by surrendering it during your lifetime. Pension schemes may provide substantial death in service provisions either by way of lump sum or pension for those who survive you. Perhaps you own a house and there is a mortgage but the mortgage debt is covered by insurance?

ARE YOU TOO YOUNG AND NOT READY TO DIE?

You might be young, fit and active and not be ready to die but the choice is not yours. Accidents do happen: young people are frequently killed in motor accidents for which they are not responsible and fatal diseases do not only strike down the elderly. In the real world it is not possible to say, 'It will not happen to me' and you will not be given a specific period of notice in advance as to when you must go; you will be leaving life and not employment.

IF YOU HAVE TO GO, YOU SHOULD GO YOUR WAY (OR TRY TO)

The right to determine how to dispose of your body after your death belongs to your executor if you make a will or to the next of kin if you do not make a will. Legally your personal wishes may be ignored, but in practice they are more likely to come to light and be carried out if you record them in a will.

THEY ARE YOUR CHILDREN AND YOU SHOULD DECIDE WHO SHALL BRING THEM UP

If you die without making proper provision for the appointment of a guardian for any children you have who are under the age of 18, they could be brought up by people you consider to be totally unsuitable, and if you are their only surviving parent, the children could even be taken into care. You cannot even rely upon your spouse or partner to care for them; he or she could die in or as the result of the same or a subsequent accident or die of an illness while they are still under age. If you make a will you can choose your children's guardian and who is to bring them up, as long as you do not try to displace a guardian appointed by a court, the children's mother or a father who was married to you at the time of their birth or has been registered in the United Kingdom as the father or a person who has been officially granted guardianship by you. However, a provision in a will can even displace such a mother, father or civil partner if, when you die, the children have been living with you under a residence order made by a court.

The ability to appoint a guardian by will is especially important to unmarried mothers because on the death of an unmarried mother, her children's father does not necessarily have the legal powers of a parent or become their guardian.

HASN'T THE GOVERNMENT TAKEN ENOUGH TAX FROM YOU IN YOUR LIFETIME?

If you consider that you have been heavily taxed so far and paid more than your fair share or that you are not rich enough to pay death duties, then you (or your loved ones) may have a very unpleasant surprise. In today's world if you own your house and have a mortgage protection, endowment or life policy, you could well find that you have an inheritance tax problem. Remember that the value of these items and anything else which you own will be added together and that if the total is over the exemption limit (sometimes known as the nil rate band and which at the present date is £275,000) the excess will be taxed at a full 40 per cent! It is true that what your civil partner or spouse inherits from you is free from inheritance tax on your death, but that does not necessarily help in that it will only be added to whatever your spouse or partner owns and compound the problem when he or she dies. Moreover, the exemption does not apply to cohabitees unless they have a registered civil partnership. By making a will and carefully considering its provisions you may be able to arrange matters so that more of your estate is inherited by those you care for and less by the state.

SPARING YOUR NEXT OF KIN EXTRA PAIN

Your next of kin might be just too upset to deal with your business affairs when you die or you might not wish them to handle your business.

It is only natural that those close to you will be upset when you die and having to repeatedly deal with papers relating to you will only make matters worse.

Your next of kin may not have sufficient business knowledge or ability to handle your affairs, and if they are complicated you might wish to entrust them to a professional executor or knowledgeable and experienced friend. If you have few close relatives and do not have contact with them, do you really wish a long-lost cousin to wind up your financial affairs for you after your death or would you prefer a trusted friend or business colleague to do it for you? Again on death you might wish to place your affairs in the hands of your principal beneficiaries or a combination of several of the above. Making a will gives you the flexibility in these matters which anyone dying intestate does not have.

SOME MATTERS REALLY ARE URGENT

Executors derive their powers from the will itself and they come into effect at the moment the person who made it dies. If a valid will has not been made, no one has any legal power to act until someone (who is called an administrator and who is usually the next of kin) has been appointed to do so by a document called Letters of Administration issued by the High Court. The appointment takes some time. Delay can be disastrous if there are matters requiring urgent attention; for example, you may have been negligently killed in an accident and have a legal right to claim for damages which will fail if the claim is not made within specified time limits, or there might be a family dispute concerning the funeral arrangements or who is to make them.

WHAT HAPPENS IF YOU DIE WITHOUT A VALID WILL (IN GREATER DETAIL!)

If you die without making a will you are said to die intestate and your estate will be wound up and inherited according to intestacy law.

Who will administer your estate?

Unless your estate is under £5,000 after paying your funeral expenses and debts, or it consists entirely of property held in joint names as joint tenants (as to which see Chapter 3), it will be necessary for someone to be appointed as the administrator of your estate by the Probate Registry at the High Court and given powers to wind it up in accordance with intestacy law. This is done by the Registry granting Letters of Administration of the estate to the appropriate person. You have no right to decide who that person will be. The following people have the right to ask to be appointed and they are entitled in the order set out:

1. Your spouse or civil partner, or if he or she has survived you but dies before obtaining Letters of Administration of your estate, his or her personal representative.
2. Your children or other issue, i.e. children or grand-children or other descendants.
3. Your father and mother.
4. Your brothers and sisters of the whole blood or their issue.
5. Your brothers and sisters of the half blood or their issue.
6. Your grandparents.
7. Your uncles and aunts of the whole blood or their issue.
8. Your uncles and aunts of the half blood or their issue.
9. The Crown.
10. Your creditors.

Only blood relations and adopted or illegitimate relatives count, not relatives by marriage.

Who will inherit your estate?
A few general points first.

Again, except for your spouse or civil partner, only blood relationships and adopted or illegitimate relatives count, not relations by marriage.

The law as to who will inherit your estate if you die intestate divides your relatives into groups or classes according to their relationship to you, e.g. children, siblings, grandparents, etc. All members of a given class inherit in equal shares. If a member of one class has died before you and leaves issue who survive you, the issue inherit equally between them the share which their predeceasing parent would have inherited had he survived you. There is a specific order in which the various classes inherit and if all members of a given class have died before you without leaving issue who survive you, the next class inherits. The words 'child' and 'children' are used to mean your immediate descendants (as opposed to grand-children) and the word 'issue' is used to mean all your descendants. If those entitled to inherit are under the age of 18, the inheritance is held in trust for them until they either reach the age of 18 or enter into a registered civil partnership or marry under that age. If your civil partner or spouse does not survive you by 28 days your estate is distributed as if he or she had not survived you. Net estate means the estate after deducting all debts, liabilities, inheritance tax and funeral and testamentary expenses.

To decide who will be entitled to inherit your estate when you die it will be necessary to look for the first class and if there is no member of that class who survives you or predeceases you leaving issue who survive you, to move on to the next class.

The first person to have a claim on your estate will be your civil partner or surviving spouse and the amount to which he or she will be entitled will depend upon the size of the net estate and whether or not there are any surviving issue or certain other close relatives. If your spouse or registered civil partner survives, but for a period of less than 28 days beginning on the day on which you die, he or she is considered not to have survived you.

If you leave a surviving spouse or civil partner but no issue and no parent, brother or sister of the whole blood or issue of a brother or sister of the whole blood, your spouse or civil partner will inherit the entire estate.

If you leave a surviving spouse or civil partner and issue or any of the specified relatives, your spouse or civil partner will be entitled to your personal chattels, i.e. moveable items such as sporting trophies or motor car, but personal chattels does not include items used in any business, e.g. a delivery van.

Your spouse or civil partner is also entitled to be paid a fixed sum of money known as a statutory legacy out of your estate and interest on the statutory legacy at the rate of 6 per cent from the date of death until the administrator of your estate pays it to her.

If you are survived by issue your spouse's or partner's statutory legacy is £125,000. If you leave no surviving issue but leave a surviving parent, or a brother or sister of the whole blood or issue of a brother or sister of the whole blood who has died before you, the legacy is £200,000.

Your surviving spouse or civil partner will also be entitled to one half of what is known as 'the residuary estate', i.e. what remains of the net estate after deducting the personal chattels and the statutory legacy. If you also leave surviving issue, your civil partner or spouse will be entitled to the share of the residuary estate only during her lifetime, but if you leave no surviving issue, then your spouse or civil partner is entitled to the share for her use and benefit absolutely. When your spouse or partner is only entitled to the half share of the residuary estate for the remainder of her life, then because it has to be left for those who are entitled to inherit it after her death, she can only spend the income that share produces and cannot spend the capital sum represented by the share. Where your spouse or civil partner is entitled to the share for her own use and benefit absolutely she can, of course, dispose of both the capital and income as she wishes.

Your surviving spouse or civil partner is entitled to require your personal representative to use the remaining residuary estate to purchase her interest for life in the one half share of your residuary estate from her. If your home is freehold or leasehold with at least two years of the lease to run at the date of your death, your spouse or civil partner can also insist upon using her share of the residuary estate to buy the home, paying any difference in value in cash. To exercise either of these two rights your spouse or partner must give notice of her intention to do so to your personal representatives within a year of the issue of the grant of Letters of Administration of your estate. If your spouse or civil partner is your sole personal representative the notice should be given to The Senior Registrar of The Family Division of The High Court of Justice. In cases where the home

- is part of a building or agricultural estate contained in the residuary estate or
- is used in part or entirely as a hotel or lodging house or

◆ in part for other than domestic purposes

the right cannot be exercised unless a court is satisfied that it is not likely to diminish the value of the other assets in the residuary estate or make them more difficult to dispose of.

If you leave a surviving spouse or civil partner and issue, the issue will inherit one half of the residuary estate on your death and the other one half of the residuary estate after the death of your surviving spouse or partner.

If you leave a surviving spouse or civil partner but no issue, she will inherit one half of the residuary estate for her own use and benefit absolutely and the other one half share of the residuary estate is inherited by your parent if one survives you and if both survive you then by them in equal shares, or if no parent has survived, by your brothers or sisters of the whole blood and issue of deceased brothers and sisters of the whole blood, the issue of your deceased brothers or sisters inheriting equally between them the share which their deceased parent would have taken had he survived you.

If you leave no surviving spouse or civil partner but leave issue the issue inherit the net estate.

If you leave no surviving spouse or civil partner and leave no issue but leave a parent or parents who survive you, the net estate is inherited by your parent, and if both survive you, then by them equally.

If you leave no spouse, civil partner, issue or parent, the net estate is inherited by the following classes of people who are living at your death and in the following order so that if there is no one in a class living at the death the subsequent class inherit, namely your brothers and sisters of the whole blood, or if none, your brothers and sisters of the half blood, or if none, your grandparents, or if none, your uncles and aunts of the whole blood, or if none, your uncles and aunts of the half blood.

If you leave none of the above the estate goes to the Crown, the Duchy of Cornwall or Duchy of Lancaster.

A person considered to be your spouse for the purposes of the laws of intestacy when once you have married them until a decree absolute (not a decree nisi) of divorce or nullity or a judicial separation (other than in the magistrates court) has been made in respect of the marriage and to be your civil partner from when the partnership is registered until it is dissolved.

Your children will only have a right to their inheritance under the above provisions when they attain the age of 18 or enter into a registered civil partnership or marry under that age, whichever happens first, but there are provisions for the administrator of the estate to use up to one half of a child's potential share for the child's benefit before the relevant event occurs.

'Children' does not include stepchildren under the law as to inheritance on intestacy. Adopted children inherit on intestacy from their adoptive parents but not from their natural parents.

For the purpose of inheritance, if you are an unmarried mother and you conceive a child artificially i.e. by fertilisation by a donor, as the result of treatment provided for you and the man together, the donor of the sperm is considered to be the father of the child; if you are married and not judicially separated and you conceive a child artificially, your husband is considered to be the father of the child, unless it is proved that he did not consent to the fertilisation. These rules do not apply to inheritance of a title or land which devolves with the title.

What will happen to your business?

Under the general law your executors, or your administrators if you do not make a will and die intestate, have power to carry on the business without restrictions on that power, only for the purpose of winding it up and that should be done within one year. To do so might be impractical or economically disadvantageous. If they take longer than a year your personal representatives can be held liable in law for any debts and losses incurred. If you run or are likely to run a business and you make a will you can provide in the will that your executors shall have power to carry on the business either alone or in partnership and provide that they shall be entitled to be indemnified out of the business for any debts or liabilities reasonably incurred in so doing.

Have I convinced you that you need a will?
Then do not delay. Let us make one now before it is too late.

Can You Make a Will and How to Do It

CAN YOU MAKE A WILL?

To be entitled to make a will you must have valid testamentary capacity. This means that, in addition to being over the age of 18 (unless you are seaman at sea or you are in the armed forces and on active military service), you must be able to

◆ understand roughly what making a will means, i.e. the nature of the transaction you are entering into;

◆ be capable of having a rough idea of what you have to leave;

◆ be aware of those you have a moral obligation to benefit and those you are benefiting in the will; and

◆ understand in broad terms the effect of the will.

You may have testamentary capacity and be able to make a valid will even though you are of unsound mind and suffering from delusions in some respects, as long as that insanity does not affect the above points. For example, you may have good testamentary capacity even though you are convinced that the world is a cube.

Your will will not become invalid if you become totally insane or otherwise lose your testamentary capacity after making it, as long as you had testamentary capacity at the time you made it. Even if you are normally mentally incapable, you are legally able to make a valid will in any lucid period.

If you ask someone else, for example a solicitor, to prepare a will for you, the will will be valid if you had testamentary capacity at the time you gave the instructions for the preparation of the will, even if it is doubtful whether you had testamentary capacity at the time you signed the will, provided that at the time you signed the will you understood that it put into effect the instructions which you had given for the will.

If you do not have testamentary capacity the Public Guardianship Office can be asked to arrange for a judge having powers under the Mental Health Act 1983 to make a will for you provided that you are over the age of 18. Such a will is known as a statutory will and is to benefit those for whom you might be expected to benefit if you were not mentally disordered. Although an application for the making of a statutory will is expensive, it might be justified for the reasons set out in Chapter 1, especially if there have been major changes in tax laws or your financial or other circumstances since you lost your capacity, or made your previous will. The Power of the Guardianship Office to make a will includes power to revoke an existing will. The Public Guardianship Office can be contacted at Archway Tower, 2 Junction Road, London N19 5SZ, tel 0845 330 2900, fax 020 7664 7715.

If your will is rational on the face of it at the relevant time there will be a rebuttable presumption that you had full testamentary capacity when you made it. If your capacity is likely to be challenged it might be sensible to ask your doctor to examine you and to witness the will.

The fact that you are unable for physical or educational reasons to read or write or that you can only sign your name by making your mark does not prevent you from making your will; these difficulties can be dealt with in the wording of the will as we shall see later.

If you have the necessary mental capacity and are a member of the armed forces engaged in actual military service or are a seaman at sea, then notwithstanding the fact that you may be under the age of 18, you can make an informal will which will not be revoked by merely leaving the service or, in the case of a seaman, returning to land.

FORMALITIES

Members of the armed forces engaged in actual military service and seamen at sea can make informal wills without observing any formalities whatsoever: their wills can be made irrespective of their age, do not have to be witnessed and need not be made in writing. Unless you fall within those categories there are some formalities which must be observed if your will is to be valid and legally enforceable.

The remainder of this chapter applies to any will that you make in England or Wales. The formalities for making wills while you are abroad or for making what are known as 'international wills' are dealt with in Chapter 7.

The formalities, which are legally required and are essential in respect of wills which you make in England or Wales, are as follows.

YOUR WILL MUST BE MADE IN WRITING

Your will can be in any form of writing, handwritten, typed or printed, and in any language, but it *must be in writing* and any other expression of your wishes will not be effective. Oral expressions of your wishes and wills recorded on sound-tapes or videotapes are therefore not valid wills.

Your will should be written *legibly* because what cannot be read cannot be enforced. You do not necessarily have to write out the will yourself but if a beneficiary writes out the will by hand for you, suspicions might arise as to whether or not you knew of and approved of the contents of the will when you signed it and it could be challenged.

Your will can be written *on any material*, on paper, parchment, linen or carved in stone if you wish. Certain stationers sell 'will forms' upon which the basic parts of a will are pre-printed and on which you only have to fill in the blanks, but for some reason or another people always seem to have difficulty in filling them in correctly. In over 35 years practising as a solicitor I cannot recollect seeing more than a dozen will forms which had been correctly completed. As in all other matters relating to wills, when considering the material upon which your will is to be written, it is better to keep it simple and use a blank sheet of good quality paper because with good luck and a healthy lifestyle it will be many years before your will will be required to be proved! If you use ink, use permanent ink. Although to do so would not make your will invalid, for reasons of security do not use pencil or a writing media which can be easily erased. Not everyone is honest in financial matters!

YOUR WILL MUST BE SIGNED BY YOU OR BY SOMEONE IN YOUR PRESENCE AND AT YOUR REQUEST

The signature need not be your full name or indeed your name at all as long as a court will be satisfied that the mark which is made was intended as your signature and that it was intended to authenticate the document as your will. I always told clients to sign their will in the same way as they would sign their cheques on the basis that if the mark intended as a signature can extract money from their bank account it can do anything! An inked thumbprint has been held by a court to be a sufficient signature, as has the testator's initials impressed by his seal, but the courts have not yet accepted electronic signatures and it is best to keep it simple and avoid courts rather than tempt fate by using such esoteric forms of authentication.

In whatever way your will is signed, it must either be done by you personally or by someone for you, at your direction and in your presence. To avoid problems, you should always sign your will personally or at least make a mark as your signature if you possibly can. If you are physically unable to sign or make your mark, e.g. because of paralysis or because you are blind, you can ask someone to sign the will for you as your will but they must do so in your presence and in the presence of the required witnesses.

YOUR SIGNATURE ON THE WILL MUST BE MADE OR ACKNOWLEDGED BY YOU IN THE PRESENCE OF TWO OR MORE WITNESSES WHO MUST BE PRESENT AT THE SAME TIME

If all the witnesses to your will are not with you when the will is signed, you must confirm to them that the signature is yours and all the witnesses must be there when you do so. It is not sufficient for you to confirm it to each witness on separate occasions or for you to sign in the presence of one or more witnesses when the others are not there and subsequently to confirm the signature to the absent witness or witnesses.

Although the Wills Act 1837 refers to two or more witnesses it is only necessary and usual to have two witnesses to your signature, but they must be of age and mentally capable.

EACH WITNESS MUST SIGN THE WILL AND EITHER SIGN OR ACKNOWLEDGE HIS SIGNATURE IN YOUR PRESENCE

You must be present when the witness signs or acknowledges his signature, but there is no necessity for each witness to be present when the other witness signs.

IT MUST BE APPARENT THAT YOU INTEND TO GIVE EFFECT TO THE WILL BY SIGNING IT

In practice your signature and those of the witnesses should appear at the end of the will to show that they are intended to give effect as your will to all that goes before the signatures. If words appear in the will after the signatures there can be problems in that the Probate Registry will insist on the witnesses swearing an affidavit or making an affirmation to confirm that the words were in your will when it was signed and not added later by you or by anyone else and the witnesses might not then be alive, traceable or able to recollect. If the words were added later, of course, they would be ineffective and invalid and would not be admitted to probate.

If there are more pages than one it is as well for yourself and the witnesses to also sign at the bottom of each page so that nothing can be added later to the page and for the pages to be numbered so that no further pages can be inserted.

It is usual to indicate in the wording of the will that the document is signed as your last will. See the specimen will in the appendix.

A FEW GENERAL WORDS ON THE SUBJECT OF SIGNING THE WILL AND WITNESSES

The witnesses are witnessing your signature. It follows therefore that you must sign first or there will be nothing for them to witness. The witnesses must be in a position to see you sign, not blind and their view must not be obscured. The witnesses need not know the contents of the will or even that it is a will, because it is your signature that they are witnessing and not the document.

When are you and the witness in each other's presence? When each can see what the other is doing, even if you are not in the same room.

All the above requirements as to the witnessing of wills might seem complicated but if you ensure that

◆ yourself and two adult witnesses are all present in the same room before any signing begins

◆ the witnesses are not blind

◆ the witnesses are not beneficiaries or the executors of the will or the spouse or civil partner of any beneficiary or executor (if they are the will will be valid but the beneficiary will lose the bequest and the executor possibly his right to expenses unless specifically authorised to charge them or the will is an informal military one or a seaman's will made at sea)

◆ the witnesses are likely to be traceable if required when you die

◆ you sign first followed by each witness

◆ each witness signs with his usual signature and follows it by his printed name and his address and occupation or status (married woman, widow, etc.) if a woman and

◆ no one leaves the room before the signing is complete

there should be no problem.

CONVENTIONS

There are other traditional practices which, while they are not legal requirements and will not invalidate your will if they are not followed, are conventions used in the layout of wills and which will give your will a classy, professional appearance. These are as follows:

Format

1. The will should be laid out in paragraphs numbered in sequence after a first paragraph which confirms the nature of the document (will or codicil) and states your name, address and occupation or, if you are a woman without an occupation, your status (married woman, widow etc.). The first words of each paragraph should be in block capitals and underlined.

2. The order of the paragraphs should be

   a) a clause beginning <u>I REVOKE</u> to revoke all previous testamentary dispositions if that is your intention;

   b) a clause beginning <u>I APPOINT</u> which deals with the appointment of executors and trustees;

   c) a clause beginning <u>I GIVE</u> which sets out any legacies of money which you might wish to make;

   d) a clause beginning <u>I BEQUEATH</u> which sets out any gifts of specific articles which you wish to make;

   e) a clause beginning <u>I DEVISE</u> which sets out any gifts of freehold land or buildings;

   f) a clause beginning <u>I GIVE DEVISE BEQUEATH AND APPOINT</u> which deals with any remaining property you may have to dispose of;

   g) separate clauses or sub-clauses giving your executors additional powers or excluding powers which the law gives them by default;

h) a clause beginning <u>I EXPRESS</u> the wish, which sets out your wishes in relation to your funeral and the disposal of your body after your death;

i) a clause beginning <u>IN WITNESS</u> explaining that you have signed your will and stating the date on which it is signed unless the date has been stated in the introductory paragraph; and finally

j) a clause called an attestation clause that explains the circumstances in which the will was signed and witnessed beginning <u>SIGNED</u>. If you are unable to read this clause should explain that the will had been read over to you before you signed it and the two witnesses then signed it in your presence. In these circumstances it should also state that you understood and approved the will. If you are unable to sign the will, the clause should explain that it is signed by a named person for you, at your request and in the joint presence of yourself and two witnesses, who then signed the will in your presence and the presence of the person who signed for you. Suitable forms of attestation clause can be found in the appendix to this book.

3. All names should be set out in full, in capitals and underlined.

4. Sums of money should be stated in words in underlined block capitals followed by the sum in brackets in figures.

Reference to the specimen wills in the appendix to this book will make the above points clearer.

PRECAUTIONS AGAINST FRAUD

As a precaution against the possibility of subsequent tampering with the will and fraud:

1. The date of the will should be expressed in words rather than figures (words are more difficult to alter than figures) and any sums of money should be expressed in words followed by the sum in brackets expressed in figures.

2. Each page of the will should be numbered and signed by you and by the witnesses as close to the last line on the page as possible to prevent anything being inserted.

3. Try to avoid making any alterations, interlineations or obliterations, but if they are unavoidable, yourself and the witnesses should each write his or her respective initials as close as possible to them to authenticate them.

4. The gaps at the end of each line and paragraph should be ruled through.

5. The same pen should be used by you and by the witnesses when signing to indicate that all signed at the same time.

6. If you are blind or otherwise unable to read, have someone other than the person who prepared the will read it over to you before it is signed.

Finally never, never attach, pin or fasten anything to the will, even with a paperclip.

$$\left(3\right)$$

What Can be Left in Your Will?

GENERAL PRINCIPLES

The law as to whether or not you can leave moveable property (i.e. anything other than land, which includes non-portable buildings on land) by your will is decided by the law of the state in which you are domiciled, i.e. the state which is considered to be your permanent home at the date of your death. The law as to whether or not you can leave immoveable property by your will is the law of the state in which the land is situated.

At birth you have the same domicile as your mother if you are illegitimate or your father is dead, otherwise the domicile of your father. This is known as your domicile of origin. You can exchange your domicile of origin for what is known as a domicile of choice by abandoning your ties with the state in which you have your domicile of origin and moving to live in another state *with the intention of making it your permanent home.* A new domicile of choice can be acquired as frequently as you wish, but you can only have one domicile at any given time. Those who are mentally incapable or under the age of 16 have the domicile of the person upon whom they are dependent and their domicile will follow any change in that person's domicile. This is known as a domicile of dependency. A woman who married before 1 January 1974 acquired her husband's domicile by virtue of the marriage, but after that date she can change it and her domicile is no longer dependent upon her husband. There are exceptions to the above rules for inheritance tax purposes, in that for those purposes,

◆ you are deemed to retain your domicile in the relevant part of the United Kingdom for three years after leaving it and

◆ you are deemed to be domiciled here if you have been resident here for any part of 17 or more of the 20 preceding *tax* years.

I use the word 'state' in connection with domicile rather than 'country' because domicile is defined not by national boundaries but by places which have their own independent system of law.

If your domicile is England and Wales you can dispose by will of anything in England and Wales and any moveable property which you have abroad and you can dispose of it to whom you wish and to the exclusion of your family unless

◆ you have restricted yourself by contract, e.g. by entering into an agreement to create and not revoke mutual wills; or

◆ it is something which does not pass to your personal representative on your death, e.g. jointly owned property held as joint tenants; or

◆ it is a contract in which your personality is an essential element, e.g. a contract to paint a portrait or to write a book; or

- it is property you do not own (e.g. assurance policies taken out by you on trust for another) and over which you have not been given a power of appointment; or

- the property has been 'nominated' and the nomination has not been revoked; or

- it is property the disposal of which is restricted by its nature, e.g. some rights in immoveable property such as a personal licence or permission to use or cross the land of another, or shares in some small companies; or

- it is your body; or

- statute law restricts your right to dispose of it in the way you wish.

Some of these matters are easy to understand but I will deal with the others in more detail.

MUTUAL WILLS

Mutual wills must not be confused with so called 'mirror wills'.

Mirror wills are merely wills each of which precisely reflects or mirrors the terms of the other and are frequently entered into by husband and wife. They are nothing more than wills with reciprocal terms. Mutual wills are wills made by one testator under a legally binding contract with another testator to make the wills and not revoke them without the other's consent. The contract need not be a written one unless the will disposes of an interest in land.

To be a legally binding contract the agreement must

+ be intended to create a legally binding relationship;

+ have an element of bargain, i.e. of a mutual exchange of promises.

The fact that two people make their wills together at the same time and in identical terms does not by itself make them mutual wills. To be mutual wills there must also be further evidence of a legal contract to make the bequest and not revoke it without the beneficiary's consent. Extrinsic evidence, i.e. evidence which is not apparent from the wills themselves (e.g. letters exchanged between the parties concerned), can be used to show that what on the face of it appear to be mirror wills were in fact mutual wills. In appropriate circumstances, to avoid problems, you should consider including in the wills the following clause '(*insert name of other party concerned*) and I agree that our respective wills are/are not mutual wills and that each of us is/is not free to dispose of his/her property in any way he or she thinks fit in the future.' Only one of the alternatives should, of course, be included.

Makers of mutual wills need not necessarily confer benefits upon each other by their wills, provided that the agreement and the above elements of a contract are present. For example, A and B might agree that A will give up A's house and go to live with and act as a carer for B for the remainder of their joint lives, if B will leave B's house to A by will and not revoke the gift and further that A will leave the house to B's children in A's will. Another example of mutual wills would be if two partners in a business mutually agree to leave their share in the business each to the other by their wills and not to revoke the bequests.

In English law a will cannot be made irrevocable, but if one party to an agreement for mutual wills breaks the agreement, the other party is released from it and free to make alternative provisions in that other party's will.

If one party to a mutual wills agreement dies having carried out his part of the bargain and the other party makes a new will in breach of the agreement, then upon the death of the party who has broken the agreement a court would ensure that the agreement is carried out either by imposing a trust upon his estate to achieve justice for the aggrieved party's estate or granting damages in favour of the aggrieved party's estate against the other estate.

Although the law will not usually enforce a promise made in your lifetime to make a gift by your will and your executor cannot legally carry it out unless it is contained in a valid will or codicil or a binding contract to make mutual wills, the law will very exceptionally enforce such a promise if the potential beneficiary relies upon it to his detriment in such circumstances that the promise would bind you in all conscience to do no other than to carry out your promise. The essential factors which must be present are the promise, reliance upon it, detriment and extremely seriously unconscionable conduct.

JOINTLY OWNED PROPERTY, i.e. PROPERTY NOT IN YOUR SOLE NAME

There are two ways of owning property jointly in English law, namely as joint tenants or as tenants in common. The use of the word 'tenants' has nothing to do with tenants in the sense of landlord and tenant; it is merely the same word used as a technical term to signify a different concept.

If people own property as joint tenants, the law provides that on the death of one owner, that person's share is inherited by the surviving joint owner or owners by the very act of surviving, regardless of the terms of the deceased's will or the next of kin, but a share of property which is owned as tenants in common is inherited on death as provided in the deceased's will, if there is one, or if none, then by the next of kin in accordance with the intestacy laws.

How do you know whether jointly owned property was held as joint tenants or tenants in common? Usually bank accounts, building society accounts and stocks and shares in joint names are held as joint tenants, but if there is any evidence to show that the joint owners owned separate shares of the property as opposed to each joint owner owning the entirety, the joint ownership is a case of tenancies in common. The regular sharing by the joint owners of the dividends from jointly owned shares in a company in the same unequal proportions might be an example of such evidence. Joint tenants always own the asset equally and words or actions indicating that the joint owners own unequally always means that the assets are held as tenants in common. Partnerships almost invariably own property as tenants in common. When husbands and wives own property jointly they usually, but not necessarily, do so as joint tenants and not tenants in common.

Because you cannot leave your entitlement in property which you co-own as a joint tenant by will, if you wish to do so you must first sever the joint tenancy to create a tenancy in common and then leave your share by your will. A form of document to sever a joint tenancy and create a tenancy in common is included in the appendix of forms to this book and when completed must be given to the other joint tenant(s) to be effective. It is a wise precaution to arrange for the other co-owner(s) to sign a receipt to confirm that they have received the document and to place the receipted copy of the document with the title documents. If the property has a title which is registered at HM Land Registry, the receipted copy should be sent to the Land Registry at the District Land Registry (which you will find noted on your official copy of the Land Registry title document) for noting in the Registry's records. When communicating with the Land Registry you should quote the Land Registry Title Number which appears in the copy of the Land Registry title document.

Whether the jointly owned property is held as joint tenants or as tenants in common your entitlement in the property is included in the value of your estate for the purpose of calculating inheritance tax.

BUSINESS PARTNERSHIPS

If you are a partner in a business you should refer to the written partnership agreement if one exists. Partnership agreements frequently provide that on the death of a partner, the surviving partners shall have a right to buy his share, or less frequently, that the deceased partner's share shall accrue to the surviving partners without payment. Such provisions will obviously restrict your right to leave your share in the partnership to whom you wish.

If there is no written partnership agreement, then on your death the partnership will cease and the business should be wound up. Your estate will be entitled to your share of the partnership assets or the proceeds that their sale produces and they can be left by your will.

PROPERTY YOU DO NOT OWN

Insurance policies taken out or held on trust for another

It is possible when taking out an insurance policy to stipulate that the policy is taken out on trust for, i.e. for the benefit of, another person or people. It is similarly possible to make a written declaration in respect of an existing policy that the policy shall be held on trust for others. The main advantages of following these procedures are that on death or maturity the proceeds of the policy do not form part of your estate and consequently they are:

◆ immediately payable to the trustees upon production of proof of death without waiting for a grant of probate of your will or letters of administration of your estate being issued by the Probate Registry;

◆ not subject to inheritance tax.

Because the policy is held on trust and is not beneficially owned by you, it is not yours to leave and cannot be included in your will.

Other property you do not own over which you have a power of appointment

Sometimes a deed, another person's will or a trust, while it does not give you property, will give you a right (i.e. power) to decide who shall have the property. This is called a *power of appointment*. The document which gives you the power usually states whether you can use the power by deed in your lifetime or by will or by deed or will.

Other property you do not own over which you have no power of appointment

Although it might seem to be stating the obvious, you should always check that you do in fact own property you purport to give away in your will. It is easy to believe that you own articles which you have on hire purchase which in fact you only hire and are actually owned by the finance company, or consider that you own an assurance policy which you took out on trust for your wife or children. Similarly you may look upon the holiday cottage you inherited from grandmother as your own and after many years forget that she only left it to you for the duration of your life and that her will provided that thereafter it was to go to a favourite grandson. If you try to leave it by your will to your daughter and you leave a legacy to the grandson, the result will be something that you almost certainly do not expect. There is a rule in English law known as the doctrine of election to the effect that a person who accepts a benefit conferred by a document must also accept every other provision of that document and give up any other right he possesses which is inconsistent with the document. Thus if a testator who does not own something purports to give it away by his will and also gives a bequest to the true owner of the asset, the true owner must either refuse his bequest or give up his own property or its value in compensation to the other beneficiary. Therefore, in the above example, the grandson will have to decide whether he will refuse the legacy or alternatively accept it and give up the cottage (or the value of the cottage) to your daughter.

NOMINATED PROPERTY

There have been various Acts of Parliament which authorised those who deposited money with certain organisations, e.g. National Savings and Friendly Societies, to 'nominate' people to receive the deposits on the depositor's death. Such nominations are not overridden by the provisions of a will, and although it is no longer possible to make new nominations, any deposits which you have made and nominated cannot be left in your will unless the nomination is revoked by signing the organisation's specified form or by your subsequent marriage, or are frustrated by the death of the nominee before your death.

PROPERTY WHICH BY ITS NATURE HAS RESTRICTED ALIENABILITY

Some existing rights in relation to land

Some existing rights for the benefit of land can only be left by will to a beneficiary to whom the land is left; for example, a right of way which you own cannot be left separately from the land or building to which it relates (unless you are giving the right by will or codicil to the owner of the land over which it exists so that it thereby ceases to exist). However, you can give a new right of way by your will to a neighbour for use with his neighbouring land.

Shares in some limited companies

Some family companies and some private companies state in their Articles of Association (the regulations which govern the running of the company) that you cannot transfer the shares in the company (sometimes except to specified members of your family), even as the result of a gift in a will, without first offering them to the other shareholders in the company. If you own shares in a small or family company you should check the position first with the company secretary before deciding to whom you will leave them in your will.

YOUR BODY

The general rule is that it is not possible to 'own' a dead body. It follows therefore that you cannot leave your body by your will although the courts have decided in a criminal case that if body parts have changed their nature as the result of skill, such as being dissected or preserved for the purpose of exhibition or teaching, they can be property and the subject of theft.

Although you cannot leave your body by will, the Human Tissues Act of 1961 and the Anatomy Act of 1984 in effect provide that if you express a wish at any time in writing or during your last illness orally in the presence of two witnesses to the effect that your body, or any part of it, shall be used for therapeutic purposes or for the purpose of medical education, research or anatomical examination, then the person having lawful possession of it (unless he has such possession only for the purpose of its interment or cremation) may authorise such use. Similarly any such person may authorise any part of your body for such use if, after making all reasonable practical enquiries, he has no reason to believe that you or your surviving spouse or relatives would object.

The coroner's prior approval is required for such use if an inquest or coroner's post-mortem may be required.

Your executors have a right and a duty to claim your body and arrange for its disposal.

More detailed information as to the disposal of your body is given in the next chapter.

STATUTORY RESTRICTIONS ON YOUR RIGHT TO LEAVE YOUR ASSETS TO WHOM YOU CHOOSE

Statutory tenancies

Certain old tenancies of private houses and housing association properties and certain tenancies of local authority houses can pass to particular members of your family on your death, but the position is very complicated and professional advice should be sought.

However, it is interesting to note that in 2002, in the case of *Ghaidan v Mendoza*, the court decided that a provision of the Rent Act 1997 which permitted a bequest of a statutory tenancy to a person living with a tenant 'as his or her husband or wife' must be construed to mean 'as if they were his or her husband or wife' and include same-sex couples to avoid contravening the provisions of the European Convention for the Protection of Human Rights and Fundamental Freedoms 1950 as set out in the Human Rights Act 1998, which provides for respect for the home and non-discrimination on the grounds of sex, race, religion or 'other status'.

The Inheritance (Provision for Family and Dependants) Act 1975, as amended

In broad terms the Act permits

- your wife or husband or civil partner

- your former wife or former husband or former civil partner who has not remarried or registered new civil partnership

- your children

- any person who was treated as a child of any marriage or civil partnership to which you have been a party

- anyone who considers that he or she was maintained by you to a material extent immediately before your death

to claim a reasonable share of your estate after your death, even if your will leaves the claimant nothing.

A different-sex partner and possibly a same sex partner (whether the partnership is registered or not) who has been cohabiting with you as if you were man and wife or civil partner for two years immediately prior to your death can claim without having to prove he or she was maintained by you.

What is meant by the word 'immediately' has to be construed in the light of all the surrounding circumstances and can have a wider meaning than might at first be thought. The case of *Gully v Dix in re Dix deceased*, which was decided by the Court of Appeal in January 2004, is a good example. The facts were that the claimant and the deceased lived together from 1974 until August 2001 when the claimant moved out because the deceased's alcoholism caused her to fear for her safety. She never returned and in October 2001 the deceased died. The court decided that in the light of their long-standing relationship and the reason for her leaving, in spite of the fact that she had been away for the three months or so before the death, she could be considered to be living in the same household and maintained by him immediately before his death and was therefore entitled to make a claim.

The High Court or a County Court exercising matrimonial jurisdiction can bar a spouse or civil partner from making a claim under the Act on or after successful proceedings for annulment of marriage, divorce, dissolution of partnership or judicial separation.

Proceedings under the Act can be brought in the County Court or in the High Court, but they must be started within six months of the issue of a grant of representation to the estate unless the claimant can satisfy the court that there were exceptional reasons for the delay.

What is a reasonable share depends upon all the circumstances of the individual case. Factors which will be considered include the size of the estate, the conduct of deceased and the parties, the needs and resources of the parties and the length of time the relationship existed. You might decide that you wish to leave a statement either in your will or in a separate note stating why you have made no, or only limited, provision for a potential claimant. A specimen statement containing some reasons which might be applicable in a particular case can be found in the specimen note contained in the appendix to this book, but other reasons might be relevant and could be included. If you leave the statement in your will, remember that when probate of your will has been granted after your death the will will be a public document and anyone can obtain a copy for a nominal charge. It is usually better to leave any such statement in a separate note and keep it with your will. Such a statement no longer has any statutory effect but in the event of any claim your executors would find it useful.

You must therefore either make reasonable provision in your will for those described above as entitled to claim against your estate or risk an expensive challenge being made to the provisions of your will.

INTANGIBLE ASSETS

Most other intangible items such as debts, patents, copyright rights, rights to sue for damages (except to

sue for defamation) and contracts to which the personality of the parties is not an essential element can be left
by will.

PRIVATE PENSION SCHEME BENEFITS

Private pension schemes frequently include benefits
relating to death in service and benefits to take effect
after the pensioner's death. Usually these matters are
decided by the rules of the scheme administered by the
trustees of the scheme outside the will and the beneficiaries are chosen by the trustees at their discretion, but the
trustees usually will give effect to the member's intentions
expressed in a statement of the member's wishes. The
advantage of these provisions is that the benefits do not
form part of the member's estate for the purpose of
calculating inheritance tax.

Matters to be Considered When Contemplating Making Your Will

JOINT WILLS

A joint will is a single document, properly completed as their wills, by two or more people who have the requisite testamentary capacity. A joint will is treated as the separate wills of those who make it and can be revoked by each party without the consent of the other or others.

I see no merit in being a party to a joint will. Do not make one. It has nothing to recommend it and is confusing and inconvenient. On first death the original will will be retained when submitted for probate.

THE NUMBER OF EXECUTORS

Your executor is the person who is charged with the responsibility of seeing that your will is carried out. This includes arranging the funeral, taking charge of the assets, proving the will in the probate registry, paying any debts including the funeral expenses, agreeing and discharging any inheritance or other tax liability, distributing the estate to the correct beneficiaries and generally winding up your financial matters.

It is sensible to appoint at least two executors in case one should die before you or refuse the appointment, or at least to appoint someone to be substituted as the executor to cover such an eventuality. If two executors are appointed, one can keep an eye on the other! In the case of land or buildings it is sometimes necessary to have two executors to enable them to act. Do not appoint more executors than necessary because probate will only be granted to the first four named executors and the greater the number of executors who prove the will, the more cumbersome the signing of withdrawal forms, receipts, deeds, etc. becomes. Personally I find two executors to be a convenient number. Co-executors have equal powers and none is senior to any other.

Separate executors can be appointed for separate parts of the estate and this can sometimes be useful if specialised knowledge is required.

WHOM SHOULD YOU CHOOSE TO BE YOUR EXECUTORS?

Beneficiaries can be executors, but executors need not be beneficiaries and your executors do not have to be chosen from the beneficiaries, although it might be a good idea to consider appointing a principal beneficiary as an executor. If you give legacies to your executors, the legacies can be made conditional upon the executors proving your will.

Your executors should be capable of and willing to undertake the considerable responsibilities involved and should be people who are likely to be around and have the time to do the work involved. Do not choose executors who are much older than yourself or who are likely to live a great distance away from you when you die.

It goes without saying that those chosen to be executors should be people you feel you can trust and you believe to be scrupulously honest because they will have complete control of your assets when you are no longer alive. The future happiness of your loved ones might very much depend upon your executors and the manner in which they administer your estate. Choose executors who are known to be in good health, stable, competent and reliable. Your executors should be strong characters who are not likely to be unduly influenced by any particular beneficiary in the exercise of any discretion entrusted to them.

The mentally ill can be appointed as executors, but they cannot act until they have recovered.

Minors can be appointed as executors, but they cannot act until they are of age.

Professionals (solicitors, banks or trust companies) are slow and will expect to be allowed to charge for their services (sometimes heftily). The Trustee Act 2000 provides that in the absence of an express clause in the will, a trust corporation is entitled to charge 'reasonable remuneration' for services it provides and a trustee who acts in a professional capacity, but is not a trust corporation and not a sole trustee, is entitled to charge 'reasonable remuneration' for services he provides, if every other trustee agrees in writing that he may be remunerated for his services. Trustee includes executor. These provisions do not apply to trustees of charitable trusts and are not totally satisfactory. It is better to insert an express clause in the will to deal with professional executors' fees and not rely upon the provisions of the Trustee Act.

Much of the work which professional executors do and charge for can be done equally well by a layperson, e.g. liaising with beneficiaries and estate agents, but if disputes are likely or in cases where complicated assets or trusts are involved it might be advisable to appoint professionals who are knowledgeable and will not be easily influenced. Sometimes it is a good idea to appoint a member of your family, who will know the family background, to act jointly with a solicitor who will be able to supply the technical expertise. However, if you appoint the partners for the time being in a firm of solicitors to be your executors or to be co-executors, that appointment will be ineffective if the firm converts to a limited liability partnership, unless the wording of the appointment clause makes it clear that the appointment is to remain effective notwithstanding the change of status of the firm. It is not sufficient to refer to the partners in the firm 'or its successors in business as at the date of my death'.

To allow executors who are not trust corporations or professional trustees to charge for their services, the will must contain an express clause to that effect, otherwise they will be allowed to receive nothing more than their out-of-pocket expenses.

Above all, ask your proposed executors and make sure that they are truly willing to be executors of your will because they are not compelled to accept the position and could refuse after you are dead and be unable to appoint others.

If all else fails you can appoint the Public Trustee to act as your executor, but he is not allowed to manage a charitable trust or a business or to administer an insolvent estate. As with any other executor he has the right to refuse the appointment and should be consulted in advance. His fees for acting will have to be paid out of the assets of your estate.

THE APPOINTMENT OF GUARDIANS FOR YOUR CHILDREN BY WILL

Guardians are people who have certain rights and responsibilities in respect of those under the age of 18. A guardian has a right to physical possession of the child (known as the ward) of whom he or she is guardian. This is useful if any attempt to made to abduct the child. The guardian also has a duty of care for the child and a duty to ensure that it is educated, but no obligation to contribute financially to the child's welfare or right to inherit from the child under the intestacy laws. A guardian is entitled to consent or refuse to the ward's adoption, marriage and medical treatment and decide upon its religion or decide that it shall have no religion.

If you have or may have a child who is under the age of 18, it is important that you should consider the appointment of a guardian for the child in your will. It is particularly important in case both parents die as a result of a common accident and in the case of single parents.

Guardianship of children is dealt with by the Children's Act 1989 as amended by the Law Reform (Succession) Act of 1995, Adoption and Children's Act 2002 and the Civil Partnership Act 2004. To have the power to appoint a guardian by will you must have 'parental responsibility' for the child. Parental responsibility means all the rights, duties, powers, responsibilities and authority which a parent of a child has in relation to the child and the child's property by law.

The following people have parental responsibility and consequently can appoint a guardian by will:

- the mother and father of a child who were married to each other at the time of the child's birth;

- the child's mother whether or not she was married to the father at the time of the child's birth;

- the father of a child who was not married to the mother at the time of the child's birth but who has been given parental responsibility by a valid parental responsibility agreement entered into with the child's mother or who has been registered as the father in England/ Scotland/Northern Ireland or Wales;

- a registered civil partner who had been granted parental responsibility in respect of the partner's partner's child;

- in relation to a child placed for adoption, the prospective adopters while the child is in their care. (The relevant Adoption Agency has parental responsibility for the child when the child is in its care.)

- a person granted parental responsibility in relation to a child by a court;

- a guardian appointed in accordance with the Act;

- a person appointed as a 'Special Guardian' by an order made under the 2002 Act. A Special Guardian is entitled to exercise parental responsibility to the exclusion of any other person except any other Special Guardian and may appoint another to be the child's guardian in the event of death of the Special Guardian. Special guardianship orders are intended to give permanence to children not considerable suitable for adoption.

Unless registered in the United Kingdom as the father, the father of a child who was not married to the child's mother at the time of the child's birth does not have parental responsibilities in relation to the child merely by being the father, but a mother and father who were not married to each other at the birth of a child may enter into a written agreement in a form prescribed by the Lord Chancellor to give the father parental responsibility. The form must be registered with the Principal Registry of the Family Division of the High Court and the signatures to the form must be witnessed by a Justice of the Peace or by an official of the Registry, or County Court or Family Proceedings (Magistrates) Court. The Principal Registry of the Family Division is at the Principal Probate Registry, 42–49 High Holborn, London WC1V 6NP.

A person who has parental responsibility or a guardian can appoint another to be the child's guardian in the event of the parent or guardian's death. The appointment must be in writing, dated and signed by the person making the appointment or (a) in the case of an appointment by will which is not signed by the testator it must be signed in the presence of and at the direction of the testator in accordance with the requirements for a valid will or (b) in any other case signed at the direction of the person making the appointment in his presence and in the presence of two witnesses who each attest the signature.

If on the death of the person making the appointment there is no person with parental responsibility for the child and no residence order in force, the appointment takes effect on the death of the person making the appointment. If on the death of the person making the appointment there is a person with parental responsibility for the child and no residence order in force, the appointment takes effect when the child no longer has anyone with parental responsibility for him.

The appointment of a guardian by will does not displace a person with parental responsibilities or a person in favour of whom a residence order has been made and takes effect when such person's rights have finished.

The appointment of a guardian by will or codicil revokes any earlier such appointment unless it is clear that the later appointment is intended to take effect as an appointment of an additional guardian.

An appointment of a guardian by will or by codicil can be terminated:

- by a court;
- by revocation of the will or codicil;
- by a dated document made by the person who made the appointment, which document is signed by the maker or signed at his direction, in his presence and in the presence of two witnesses who each attest the signature.

A written appointment of a guardian made otherwise than by a will or codicil can be terminated:

- by a court;

- by a dated document which is signed by the maker or signed at his direction, in his presence and in the presence of two witnesses who each attest the signature;

- if to take effect on death by the person who made the appointment destroying the document by which it was made with the intention of revoking it or having some other person destroy it in his presence.

A written appointment of a spouse or civil partner to be a guardian, whether or not by will or codicil, is also revoked by a divorce or annulment or dissolution as the case may be which is recognised by the laws of England and Wales unless the document which makes the appointment shows a contrary intention.

A person appointed as guardian is not obliged to accept the appointment and is entitled to disclaim the appointment in a signed written document within a reasonable time of learning that the appointment has taken effect; you should therefore obtain the agreement of the person concerned before appointing them to be the guardian of your child.

In your will you will need to consider providing for your children's maintenance. Guardians have no right to be reimbursed for anything they spend in bringing up your children unless you give them such a right by your will. You should also consider carefully whether or not the guardians should also be executors of the will and whether or not they should be the sole executors. In the absence of a clause in your will which expressly permits it, the law permits executors to use only up to one half of the capital bequeathed to a minor for the minor's benefit and if your estate is small your will should contain a clause which increases the proportion. In the case of a bequest to any under-age beneficiary, whether or not the beneficiary is your child, if the guardians are not the only executors, your will should contain a clause which authorises your executors, in their discretion, to pay money to the guardians for the minor's benefit and for the guardians to give the executors a valid receipt and discharge for any money which is paid to the guardians. Under-age beneficiaries have no power in law to give valid receipts or discharges for capital and only minors who are married can give a receipt for income.

YOUR FUNERAL AND THE DISPOSAL OF YOUR BODY AFTER YOUR DEATH

If you leave a will your executors are entitled to claim your body and have the right and duty to dispose of it and arrange the funeral. If you do not leave a will the person primarily entitled to obtain a grant of letters of administration of the estate on your intestacy is the person entitled to these rights. What happens if there are several people equally entitled on intestacy who wish to deal with the disposal of your body or your funeral differently? An Australian case suggests that because of the need to deal with these matters quickly, if one person has already made proper arrangements, for practical reasons, that person's wishes would be preferred. The same reasoning would probably apply in the event of a dispute between your executors on the subject.

Although in law the right to decide upon matters relating to your funeral and the disposal of your body is that of your personal representatives it is usual to insert a clause in your will to set out your wishes in relation to these matters. Such a clause will guide your executors who will usually comply with them as far as they are able. The clause should be kept as brief as possible.

The chances of your executors complying with your wishes can perhaps be strengthened by leaving a legacy to your executors which is made conditional upon your wishes being carried out, as long as your wishes are not unlawful!

If your body is not claimed the local authority will dispose of it, as far as possible at the expense of the estate. If the local authority disposes of your body it is not permitted to cause your body to be cremated if it has reason to believe that to do so would be contrary to your wishes.

The following notes might be of assistance when considering how you would like your body to be disposed of after your death.

If you intended to have your funeral out of England and Wales (for example in Scotland), the coroner's permission will have to be obtained at the appropriate time to take your body out of England or Wales, whether or not it has been necessary to report the death to the coroner, and you might wish to bear this in mind when leaving directions in your will for your funeral.

If you wish your body to be cremated, cremation can only take place at an authorised crematorium, but your ashes can be buried or scattered on your land or the land of another with the owner's permission or scattered at sea.

Another possibility is to have them buried in the Garden of Remembrance of the crematorium where cremation takes place or of another crematorium. Many crematoria no longer permit the scattering of ashes in the Remembrance Garden or the burial of containers; the ashes are buried directly into the soil.

Some churchyards and cemeteries have areas for the burial of cremated remains and may permit them to be buried in a container even if they are full for burial of non-cremated remains. Burial of the ashes in a family grave which is considered to be full for the purpose of non-cremated remains is sometimes permitted.

If you wish to be buried in a churchyard or cemetery and are keen to have a particular type of headstone or memorial, check that the proposed burial ground is not likely to object to the type of headstone or other memorial that you have in mind, because churches and municipal cemetery proprietors are becoming increasingly fussy as to what they will allow. 'Green' funerals in woodland burial grounds are becoming increasingly popular and the Natural Death Centre at 6 Blackstock Road, London N4 2BT, tel: 0871 288 2098, fax: 020 7354 3831, can supply useful information about these funerals.

Although burial does not have to take place in a churchyard or cemetery, it must not constitute a danger to public health or pose a pollution threat to the water supply, and if you wish to be buried anywhere but in a churchyard or a cemetery, it is as well to check first that the local and water authorities have no objection. The Department of the Environment, Farming and Rural

Affairs is able to advise. If you proposed to be buried in your garden careful thought should be given to the resale value of the property and the problem of tending the grave if the property is sold at a future date. You should also check your title deeds to ensure that they do not contain restrictions on the use of the property that prevent its use for burial purposes. Your executors will need to keep a record of the site of the burial with the title deeds because it is illegal to disturb a grave without permission from the Home Office. The date and place of the burial will also have to be notified to the Registrar of Deaths within 96 hours of the burial. Your burial must not disturb a recognised archaeological site and any grave marker, high fencing or wall or multiple burials might require planning permission.

Burial at sea can be arranged with the assistance of a professional funeral director. A licence from the Department of the Environment, Farming and Rural Affairs and a special coffin will be required. It can only take place in certain parts of the sea and the coroner's permission will be required to take your body out of the country. Such burials are expensive.

If you wish your body to be used for organ transplants it is as well to let your family know, register on the NHS Organ Donor Register and carry a donor card because organs have to be removed within a few hours of death if they are to be of use. Donor cards are available from doctors and pharmacies. The NHS Organ Donor Register's address is PO Box 14, Patchway, Bristol BS34 8ZZ.

If tissue from your body is to be donated for research it must similarly be removed promptly. A tissue bank is maintained by the Histology Department of the Peterborough District Hospital which will collect and return bodies within a 150-mile radius. They are usually kept for about 24 hours and the tissue is used for research into pharmaceutical products. This might appeal to you if you object to testing drugs on animals. The tissue bank can be contacted at Thorpe Road, Peterborough PE3 6DA, tel 01733 875892, and has a website www.tissuebank.co.uk

FACTORS TO CONSIDER WHICH MIGHT INFLUENCE YOUR CHOICE OF BENEFICIARIES

Avoiding challenges to your will

I have already mentioned the Inheritance (Provision for Family and Dependants) Act 1975 in Chapter 3 and you might consider making reasonable provision for anyone who is in a position to have a reasonable chance of making a successful claim.

Elderly beneficiaries

If your principal beneficiaries are elderly, ask yourself how much they need in addition to what they already have in their own name. There will be a limit to how much they can spend to improve the quality of their lives if they only have a short time left to them and if they leave a large estate your bequest might aggravate their inheritance tax problem. Might it be better to skip a generation and save inheritance tax? At the other end of the scale consider the effect of your bequests upon beneficiaries' social security benefits.

The matrimonial home

I advise that you endeavour to keep a roof over your spouse's head irrespective of the effect it will have on inheritance tax on her death. Too often have I seen a child whose business has got into financial difficulties decide that it would be better for mum to pass the family home to him to avoid inheritance tax on her death and incidentally allow him to use it as collateral security for the failing business. It is not worth taking the risk that your spouse could be made homeless merely to save inheritance tax and any spouse who is reasonably able to care for herself should be given independence and security by being left the matrimonial home rather than having to rely upon the goodwill of the family.

If you wish to make gifts while you are still alive in an effort to reduce the amount of inheritance tax payable on your death and you have insufficient liquid assets because your wealth is tied up in your matrimonial home, you must bear in mind the rules relating to gifts with a reservation of an interest and the income tax charge on the use of pre-owned assets. Both of these concepts are dealt with later in this chapter under the heading 'Inheritance Tax and saving tax in your will'. Possible solutions which you might wish to consider are to 'downsize', or to raise money upon the security of the matrimonial home by means of an equity release scheme such as a roll up mortgage or a home reversionary scheme.

Downsizing is to sell your property and to move into a cheaper property. A roll up mortgage is a mortgage in respect of which you are not required to make repayments until you sell the property or die. In a home reversionary scheme you sell part or the entirety of the matrimonial home or borrow against it and in either case on the understanding that you are allowed to remain in it until you sell it or you either go into long-term care or die. If you are married or have a partner, the property should be jointly owned and the roll up mortgage or equity release scheme should be entered into jointly so that the survivor of you will have the benefits.

If you propose to enter into any of these schemes you should check:

◆ that you will be able to sell and move into another suitable property without terminating the scheme if, as a result of a change in your circumstances, your existing property becomes unsuitable;

◆ whether you will incur any penalty charge if you wish to terminate the scheme early for any reason;

◆ that there is a guarantee that you (or your estate when you die) will not be required to make up any deficiency if the value of the property becomes lower than the outstanding debt; and

◆ what effect any income you receive from the scheme or from investing any capital you obtain will have on your income tax position or means tested benefits.

You should also remember that entering into an equity release scheme would possibly prevent a third party, such as a daughter or other carer, living with you. If it did not do so it would almost certainly necessitate them leaving and perhaps becoming homeless when the scheme terminated upon your death or when it became necessary to enter into care. Throughout the entire period of the scheme or of a roll up mortgage, you would remain responsible for paying council tax and maintaining and insuring the property.

If you give away cash you received under an equity release scheme it could possibly affect the chances of having care home fees paid for you in the future.

It is essential to obtain independent legal and financial advice before entering into any such arrangements and to note that legal and surveyor's fees will be charged, although some, but not all, companies will reimburse the fees if the scheme is completed.

Gifts to the young and age-contingent gifts

Are your younger beneficiaries able to handle large sums of money sensibly or should bequests to them be held on trust for them until they reach a specified age? If so, what age, and who should hold it for them, your executors or their parents? Are the parents under the influence of the children and will they give way to the children's wishes under pressure? Should the trustees be empowered in their discretion to use the income and/or the capital for the children before they reach the specified age and if so how much of the capital or income? Should use for the children be limited to use for specified purposes for them, for example for their education? The answers to these questions depend to a large extent upon the individuals concerned, but in reaching a decision there are some legal and some tax points to be borne in mind.

There is a statutory power, which can be expressly excluded or enlarged by your will, for trustees (which includes executors) to pay or apply for the benefit of minors or beneficiaries who are contingently entitled under a trust (including a will) up to one half of the capital of the funds to which they are contingently entitled. There is also a statutory power for trustees to use the income of a bequest in this way, but it is much more complicated and does not apply to all kinds of bequests. In the case of income it is better to include an express power to use the income in this way if that is what you wish.

If a bequest produces income which is not given to or used for the benefit of the beneficiary in a particular tax year (for example because the will gives it to the beneficiary only if the beneficiary fulfils a particular condition which has not yet been fulfilled and the executors do not exercise any discretion they may have to so use it), the income is added to the capital of the bequest and incurs income tax at the rate applicable to trusts (40% or 32.5% for dividend income).

Trusts for the vulnerable (minors who have at least one deceased parent and the disabled) operate under a different scheme and are taxed at the rate applicable to the beneficiary (not at the trust rate) and are able to use the beneficiary's personal tax allowances.

Remember that each trust and each person has capital gains tax allowances and every individual, irrespective of their age, has income tax allowances which allow them to have limited capital gains and income free of tax. If the executors invest the accumulated income and they later sell the investments at a profit, the net profit will be counted as the trust's gain for capital gains tax purposes and set against the trust's capital gains tax exemption. Moreover, income cannot be legally allowed to accumulate for more than 21 years.

The income from a bequest is small compared with the capital of the bequest and I consider that the best solution to overcome these problems is to leave bequests to young beneficiaries in such a way that they only inherit the capital of the bequest when they reach an age when they can be expected to be as sensible as they ever will be, and to provide that they shall be entitled to the income irrespective of their age at the time of your death, for example to say 'I leave the sum of £x to my trustees to pay or apply the income thereof for the benefit of Y absolutely irrespective of his age and as to the capital thereof for Y if he shall attain the age of 21 years'. Even if the bequest is left in this way, any capital gains which arise from the sale of investments in which the trustees invest the capital representing the legacy pending Y reaching the age of 21 will be added to any capital gains made on the disposal of any other investments made by the trustees, for example gains made on the realisation by the trustees of any investments in which the trustees have invested the funds of other bequests which are still contingent, and the gains will count towards the trust's capital gains exemption limit.

What age should you choose for a contingent gift to become an absolute one? Again this depends in part upon the people concerned and their individual circumstances, but there is a rule of law that forbids bequests under which it is not possible to ascertain for an excessively long time who is to inherit the gift. The rule is known as the rule against perpetuities and its application is complicated. It is safer to make sure that any gifts in your will are confined to people who will be ascertained within 21 years of your death, i.e. not to make gifts which are dependent upon the beneficiary reaching an age greater than 21 and not to make gifts to anyone who will be born and reach any chosen age more than 21 years from your death.

When deciding upon the allocation of your various assets between the various beneficiaries, consider giving the assets with the greatest growth potential to younger rather than older individuals because in the normal course of things they will have longer to live before inheritance tax is payable on the recipient's death.

Whenever you make bequests to minors in your will you will need to include a specific clause in your will to authorise someone to give a receipt and a good discharge to your executors for anything they pay or transfer to or for the benefit of the minor, because the law does not permit an under-age person to give a valid receipt or discharge. It is usual to provide that a parent or guardian may give the receipt and discharge and a specimen clause is provided in the appendix to this book.

Bequests to spendthrifts and bankrupts

When a person becomes bankrupt, most of his assets are taken by his trustee in bankruptcy to be used to settle his debts. If one of your chosen beneficiaries is bankrupt when you die, as much of your bequest as is necessary will be used for the benefit of the creditors and not for the beneficiary. Consequently, if one of your chosen beneficiaries is a spendthrift and likely to become bankrupt, you might decide it is better to leave your bequest to his close family rather than to him.

Although any attempt to impose a condition on a gift that the gift shall be forfeited if the beneficiary becomes bankrupt will be ineffective and the bequest will take effect free from the condition and pass to the beneficiary's trustee in bankruptcy for the benefit of the creditors, it is possible to give something to a beneficiary *until* he becomes bankrupt and then to someone else. The difference is between making an absolute gift and then taking it back if bankruptcy occurs and making a gift for a limited period until bankruptcy occurs.

A variation is to leave the gift to your executors or separate trustees on what are known as discretionary trusts, such as to pay the income to such members of a group of named people, including the spendthrift, as the trustees shall in their discretion decide until the spendthrift beneficiary becomes bankrupt or dies, whichever shall happen first and then to pass the capital to another named beneficiary or beneficiaries. Such an arrangement would not guarantee that the spendthrift would get anything, but neither would his trustee in bankruptcy.

Yet a further possible solution is to leave the bequest on what is known as a protective trust. This means that you would leave the bequest to your executors or to separate trustees, upon trust to pay the income of the bequest to your chosen beneficiary until he becomes bankrupt or dies, whichever shall happen first and then to such members of a group of named beneficiaries (which could include the spendthrift), in such proportions as the trustees shall in their discretion decide.

There is a statutory form of protective trust, the terms of which are set out in section 33 of the Trustee Act 1925 and which can be incorporated in your will by stating that the gift is to be held upon protective trusts as provided for in that section for your named beneficiary during his life or for such lesser period as you choose and state. In essence the statutory trust would ensure that if the beneficiary did anything which would deprive him of the income from the gift, e.g. if he became bankrupt, the income would be held by the trustees during his life or the lesser period for such of the named beneficiary and his spouse, children and issue (or if he had none, for such of the named beneficiary and the persons who would be entitled to the income or trust property if he were dead), as the trustees should decide.

If you use a protective trust in your will, you do of course need to state who shall have the capital of the gift after the chosen period ends.

The disadvantage of these trusts is that they are only suitable for larger bequests because it is expensive to set them up and to run them, in that running them involves investments, accounts and tax returns, and they are complicated to draft and should be drawn up by an experienced professional.

Bequests to those incapable of managing their affairs or suffering from other disabilities

If a proposed beneficiary is incapable of managing his affairs, then, unless before he became incapable he gave an enduring power of attorney appointing an attorney to deal with them for him, it will be necessary for a receiver to manage them (including your bequest) for him under the supervision of the Public Guardianship Office. This may not be what you wish.

An alternative solution is to leave the bequest upon a discretionary trust similar to the protective trust mentioned above in connection with spendthrift beneficiaries. Such a trust may also be useful for intended beneficiaries with other handicaps or disabilities. Your chosen trustees would be given the bequest upon trust to pay the income of the bequest during the handicapped person's lifetime to a group of named beneficiaries including the handicapped person, or to accumulate it and add it to the capital and in such proportions as the trustees should in their discretion decide. The discretion given to the trustees enables them to adjust payments within limits according to the beneficiary's needs and the financial limits for any social security benefits the beneficiary might be receiving. If the disabled beneficiary is entitled to at least one half of the capital and one half of the annual income of the trust as of right, the trust might qualify as a disablement trust under section 89 of the Inheritance Tax Act 1984 and receive tax advantages. A qualifying trust will be treated as an interest in possession trust and, for example, receive a full capital gains tax allowance. To qualify as a disablement trust the disabled beneficiary must also be incapable by reason of mental disorder within the meaning of the Mental Health Act 1983 of administering his property or managing his affairs, or in receipt of attendance allowance or in receipt of disability living allowance. The disadvantages are the same as those of protective trusts. Your will would also need to say what is to happen to any capital which is left on the handicapped beneficiary's death.

The Finance Act 2004 (as amended) provides that trusts for 'the vulnerable' (minors who have at least one deceased parent and the disabled) are taxed at the rates applicable to the individual beneficiaries rather than at the (usually higher) rate for trusts. To qualify for such treatment the income must be paid to or for the use of the beneficiary by 31 December following the end of the tax year in which the income arose to the trustees. Such trusts are able to use the beneficiaries' personal tax allowances. The same provisions apply to trusts for minors on the death of a parent whether the trusts come into being under the law of intestacy or the provisions of a parent's will as long as the child will become absolutely entitled when he attains his majority.

INHERITANCE TAX AND SAVING TAX IN YOUR WILL
Inheritance tax

The earlier section which dealt with gifts to the young and age contingent gifts touched upon the different tax consequences of leaving bequests to young people in different ways and there are other ways in which the tax payable by your family can be increased or decreased by your will. When making a will you should consider your family's position overall and as a single entity.

The main tax involved with death is inheritance tax and you need to have a basic understanding of how inheritance tax works and how it is calculated to enable you to decide if you can take steps by your will to minimise it.

If you have your domicile in the United Kingdom inheritance tax applies to all your non-exempt assets in whatever country they may be, but if your domicile is outside the United Kingdom the tax will only apply to those of your assets that are situated in the United Kingdom. The United Kingdom for the purpose of inheritance tax includes England, Wales, Scotland and Northern Ireland but does not include the Channel Islands or the Isle of Man. Please refer to Chapter 3 for an explanation of the meaning of domicile and where you are deemed to be domiciled for the purposes of inheritance tax.

Inheritance tax is charged upon the market value at the date of your death of everything you own and everything you have given away in the last seven years of your life which is not exempt from the tax. In addition, it is charged upon the full capital value of any trust in which you have an interest. You may deduct from the total of these figures (a) the cost of realising or administering any property outside the United Kingdom up to 50 per cent of its value, (b) your reasonable funeral expenses and (c) any debts and liabilities you have at the date of your death. The tax is calculated as a percentage of the resultant figure. The percentage is 40 per cent at the time of writing (2005).

Gifts are valued for inheritance tax purposes at the amount by which your estate is diminished as a result of the gift and not by the amount by which the donee benefits from the gift. Tax at 20 per cent will have been paid on immediately chargeable non-exempt gifts made in your lifetime if the total value of the gifts in the previous seven years exceeded the then tax threshold and you will be given credit on your death for tax which has been paid on them, but if the tax paid exceeds the tax payable on them at death, the excess is not repayable. Immediately chargeable gifts are gifts to discretionary trusts and gifts to companies.

The inheritance tax threshold is £275,000 for the tax year 2005/6, £285,000 for 2006/7 and £300,000 for 2007/8 and the amount of your estate that falls between nil and the tax threshold is known as the *nil rate band*. Inheritance tax is only payable on the value of your estate, calculated as above, which exceeds the tax threshold, the amount of your estate which is below the tax threshold being exempt.

Any non-exempt gifts you make in the seven years prior to your death will reduce the tax threshold available to set against your estate at your death.

Gifts made between two and seven years before your death are known as *potentially exempt transfers (PETS)* and in the case of such gifts only a proportion of the tax is charged, the proportion depending upon how long you survive the making of the gift.

◆ At the time of writing, if you survive the making of the gift by over seven years no inheritance tax is payable in respect of the gift.

◆ If you survive the making of the gift by between six and seven years, tax is payable in respect of the gift at 20 per cent of the death rate, i.e. at the rate of 8 per cent.

◆ If you survive the making of the gift by between five and six years, tax is payable in respect of the gift at 40 per cent of the death rate, i.e. at the rate of 16 per cent.

- If you survive the making of the gift by between four and five years, tax is payable in respect of the gift at 60 per cent of the death rate, i.e. at the rate of 24 per cent.

- If you survive the making of the gift by between three and four years, tax is payable in respect of the gift at 80 per cent of the death rate, i.e. at the rate of 32 per cent.

This reduction of the tax payable on PETS is known as taper relief.

If, to use the technical term, you reserve a benefit from the gift, that is to say retain an interest in or continue to benefit in some way from the property you give away, for example if you give away your house but

- continue to live in it at a less than a commercial rent or
- retain the right to live in it as long as you wish prior to your death or
- occupy it for the occasional holiday

you will gain no inheritance tax relief in respect of the gift and it will be counted as part of your estate when you die. The Revenue takes a strict view of what constitutes reservation of a benefit.

Various complicated schemes (usually based upon the use of trusts) have been marketed to avoid the inheritance tax liability resulting from the gifts with a reservation of an interest rules. As with any artificial arrangements which are solely for the purpose of saving of tax, you should think carefully before entering into them because they have a habit of rebounding upon the taxpayer. In his budget of March 2004 the Chancellor of the Exchequer outlined proposals for a 'free standing income tax charge' based on 'pre-owned assets' to counteract such schemes and 'the benefit people get from having free or low cost enjoyment of assets they formerly owned or provided funds to purchase.'

A 'note' was issued by the Treasury and the proposals were incorporated into law by Schedule 15 of the Finance Act 2004. What follows is largely based upon that note and the Act. To the extent that it is Crown copyright material, Crown copyright is acknowledged and it is reproduced with the general permission given by the Controller of HMSO.

The income tax charge came into force on 6 April 2005 and applies to both tangible and intangible assets and to any funds or contributions to the funds used to acquire the assets whether the funds or contributions are directly or indirectly provided.

The income tax charge is similar to the income tax charge made upon employees for benefits in kind supplied by their employers and quantifies in cash the annual benefit enjoyed. It is equivalent in the case of property to the annual rental value of the asset or in the case of other assets, the value of the asset at a rate of interest, and in each case less any payment made under a legally binding agreement for the use of the asset.

After the deduction of the amount paid for the benefit, the sum so ascertained is added to your taxable income and taxed at your top rate of tax. The first £5,000 per annum is ignored but once the £5,000 exemption is exceeded, the exemption is totally lost.

The income tax charge does not apply to the extent that:

- the asset was disposed of before 18 March 1986

- the original gift was for the maintenance of your family or within the small gifts exemption or within the inheritance tax annual gifts allowance

- the formerly owned asset is currently owned by your spouse or civil partner

- the asset still counts as an asset for inheritance tax purposes under the gift with a reservation rules

- the asset was transferred to your spouse, former spouse, civil partner or former civil partner by court order

- it is the case of an outright gift of money made more than seven years or more before the earliest date upon which you either occupied the land or had the use of the asset as applicable

- the asset was sold for cash at arm's length whether or not the parties were connected persons

- the owner of the asset was formerly the owner of the asset only by virtue of a will or intestacy which has subsequently been varied by agreement between the parties (i.e. by a deed of family arrangement, as explained in Chapter 9)

- any enjoyment is no more than incidental, including cases where an out and out gift to a family member comes to benefit the giver as a result of a change in their circumstances.

Neither does the income tax charge apply if the total tax payable in the relevant tax year does not exceed £5,000 but if it does the benefit of this exemption is lost and tax is payable on the entire sum, but just on the excess.

Former owners are not regarded as enjoying a taxable benefit if they retain an interest which is consistent with their ongoing enjoyment of the property. For example, the charge will not arise if your elderly parent formerly owning the whole of their home passes a 50 per cent interest to you and you live with them.

If you so elect on or before 31 January in the year of assessment immediately following upon the first year of assessment in which the charge applies to the property concerned you may choose to have the property concerned treated as part of your estate for inheritance tax purposes as a gift with reservation of an interest rather than have the benefit taxed as income. In those circumstances, the property will be eligible for the normal IHT reliefs and exemptions available, for example, to business and agricultural property and to heritage assets. As to these reliefs and exemptions, please see below.

Only assets in the UK are affected by the scheme imposing the income tax liability in respect of pre-owned assets if you do not have and are not deemed to have a UK domicile; if you do it applies in respect of all your assets, wherever the assets are.

If you give an asset away and pay a full commercial rent or hiring fee to use it, although doing so will save inheritance tax, it will not be an otherwise tax-efficient transaction because, as far as income tax is concerned, you will be paying the rent out of your taxed income and the recipient of the gift will have to pay income tax on the rent.

Moreover if it was your principal private residence you will lose your capital gains tax exemption for a principal private residence.

Gifts that are exempt from inheritance tax are

- gifts made more than seven years prior to your death without the reservation of an interest;

- gifts of any amount to your spouse or civil partner, unless you are domiciled in the United Kingdom but your spouse or civil partner is not, in which case the exemption is limited to £55,000;

- lifetime gifts of up to £3,000 in the tax year (any unused benefit of this exemption can be carried forward for one – but only one – year);

- regular gifts made during your lifetime which are made out of your income (not from your capital) which do not reduce your standard of living;

- wedding gifts made before the ceremony during your lifetime, up to £5,000 to your child, up to £2,500 to a grandchild and up to £1,000 in the case of anyone else;

- gifts made in your lifetime for the maintenance of your spouse, ex-spouse, civil partner, civil partner's dependent relatives and children who are under the age of 18 or are in full-time education;

- gifts to registered charities for charitable purposes;

- gifts for certain national purposes including gifts to most museums and art galleries and to political parties which have at least two sitting members of the House of Commons or which have one sitting member and whose candidates polled 150,000 votes at the last general election;

◆ gifts of land to registered housing associations.

Gifts in any number of the above classes can be made to the same person without losing the benefit of the exemption and in addition any number of gifts of up to £250 can be made in a tax year provided that no other gift has been made to the same person in the same tax year.

When you make a gift you should also consider the capital gains tax implications of the transaction.

If you are married or have a registered civil partnership arrangement remember that each spouse and civil partner has a separate set of gift exemptions.

There are reliefs in certain circumstances for some kinds of property, namely agricultural property and businesses (other than investment company or property businesses), which have been owned for at least two years prior to death, but the conditions for such relief are complex and if you think that they may apply you should seek advice from your solicitor or accountant.

Any tax which becomes payable on a PET which you make is payable primarily by the person to whom the gift is given, but if the tax has not been paid to the Revenue within 12 months of the death the Revenue can also recover it from your personal representatives out of your estate. Inheritance tax payable on an immediately charge-able transfer by way of gift which you make is payable by you unless the donee and yourself agree otherwise and if payable by you the gift must be 'grossed up', that is to say the gift is considered to be the amount of the gift and the amount of the tax payable because that is the amount by which your estate is diminished.

The wording of your will can determine who pays any inheritance tax on bequests made by the will. Unless you state otherwise in your will, tax is borne by those who inherit your residuary estate except in the case of joint or foreign property in which cases the tax is payable by the beneficiary unless your will states to the contrary.

To calculate the inheritance tax payable on a non-exempt lifetime gift, deduct the tax threshold from the value of the gift and apply the full tax rate to obtain the figure for the tax. Then apply taper relief to the resulting figure. Tax is only payable on lifetime gifts if the total of your chargeable gifts themselves exceed the tax threshold, in which case apply taper relief to the tax, not to the value of the gift.

To calculate the inheritance tax payable on your death estate, add the total of your death estate to the total of the chargeable gifts and deduct the tax threshold. Apply the full tax rate to the resultant figure and then deduct the full tax payable on the lifetime gifts (calculated as above before the application of taper relief).

I agree the above calculations are complex and if you have difficulty in following them, don't worry too much – just remember that when once your estate, calculated as above, crosses the inheritance tax exemption threshold, your beneficiaries will be paying tax at a very high rate on the excess and that any non-taxable gift you make, either in your lifetime or by your will, will only cost your estate £60 for every £100 given because the other £40 would have been payable to the Revenue as inheritance tax. It is therefore important to make the best use possible of any inheritance tax exemptions and from a tax point of view, provided you do not impoverish yourself, it is an excellent idea to give as much as you can away in your lifetime and the sooner you give it the more tax you will save. You might also have the pleasure of seeing the recipients enjoy the gifts and perhaps even make good use of them, something that it is debatable that you will be able to do after your death!

In deciding whether what you give away in your lifetime will impoverish you, do not forget the effect of inflation and remember that you cannot have your cake and eat it. To be a tax-effective gift it must go completely and you cannot retain any benefit from it, even by a behind-the-scenes arrangement. Also, when deciding which assets to give, consider giving the assets with the greatest growth potential because the asset given will be valued as at the date you make the gift and the gift of assets with the greatest growth between the date of the gift and the date of your death will bring about the greatest reduction in the value of your estate for inheritance tax purposes if you survive seven years.

If you are able to make such gifts to younger rather than older individuals, so much the better because in the normal course of things they will have longer to live before inheritance tax is payable on the recipients' death. Similarly, you should bear in mind and tend to retain assets which might receive some inheritance tax relief or exemption such as gifts of shares in unquoted companies which have been held for two years or more, some business property and agricultural property and commercial woodlands.

In the choice of which assets should be given and which retained, bear in mind which assets are exempt from capital gains tax and that there is no capital gains payable on death, so that assets on which you already have a large capital gain might be those to retain unless they can be given away under your annual capital gain exemption limit.

What you can do in your will to minimise inheritance tax

Inheritance tax is mainly a problem of the moderately wealthy: the poor are not within its range and the very rich can afford to indulge in legal tax avoidance without substantially affecting their standard of living. The principle is that if you have it when you die, you pay, but if you are only moderately well off your main financial asset is likely to be your home, and although you can leave that and most other assets you possess to your spouse or civil partner without paying any inheritance tax, to do so will only compound the problem when your spouse or partner dies, in that what you leave and she does not dispose of before her death will be added to assets already in her name and further exceed the nil rate band, thus incurring 40 per cent tax. On the other hand, if you are only moderately well off, your surviving spouse or civil partner will need your house and other assets to live reasonably comfortably after you die and you cannot easily give them to others before your death or by your will if you have a spouse or civil partner.

If you have no spouse or civil partner, the exemption will not apply and the entirety of your non-exempt estate which you retain until your death and which is over the tax threshold will be taxed, subject to any available reliefs. You cannot give it all away – you do need to keep something back to live on!

Lifetime gifts by terminally ill spouses and civil partners

If one spouse or partner becomes terminally ill, try to make use of exempt lifetime gifts to the maximum as each tax year progresses and use the fact that lifetime gifts between spouses or registered civil partners are exempt from both inheritance and capital gains taxes to ensure that any estate of the spouse or partner who is likely to die first which is not to be left to the survivor will exceed the exempt threshold by as little as possible; the survivor can then use his own lifetime gift exemptions to make gifts from the excess to the intended beneficiaries which would have been taxable if made on the first death.

Equalisation of estates between spouses, civil partners, the survivor exemption and the nil rate band

If you are in a happy marriage or civil partnership and believe that you are likely to remain so, then because there is usually no means of knowing which spouse or partner will be the first to die, the most obvious and effective way to reduce the amount of inheritance tax payable on your death and the death of your partner or spouse is to equalise your taxable estates during your joint lives by the richer making gifts to the other and for each of you to make use of the survivor exemption and the nil rate band. You do this by leaving value up to the nil rate band to beneficiaries other than your spouse or partner and the remainder of your estate to the spouse or partner. Whether or not you can afford to do so will depend upon the total value of your joint estates, the state of your marriage or civil partnership and the standard of living each of you are accustomed to and are prepared to accept.

However, in considering how to equalise the estates and whether or not it will be sensible to equalise the estates, as always, bear in mind the effect on your income tax positions. From an income tax point of view, it is best, as far as possible, to ensure that both parties make equal use of their lower and basic rate income tax bands and this might decide which party shall hold which assets and indeed whether and to what extent you should equalise your assets to help with inheritance tax planning.

Let us compare the positions if you and your wife or partner make use of the survivor exemption and the nil rate band and if you do not.

Suppose that you and your wife or partner have a total estate between you valued, after payment of the funeral expenses, at £510,000, of which £230,000 is made up of the unmortgaged matrimonial home.

If everything is in your name and you die first and leave all your estate to your widow or civil partner no inheritance tax will be payable on your death because everything you leave to the survivor is exempt (the survivor exemption).

On the survivor's subsequent death the first £275,000 of the estate will be exempt from tax because it does not exceed the tax threshold. The remaining £235,000 will incur tax at the rate of 40 per cent, i.e. £94,000 tax will be payable and the beneficiaries will inherit £416,000 of the £510,000 estate.

If the joint estate had been equalised so that each party held £255,000, on your death you could leave your share of the matrimonial (£115,000) to your wife or partner which would be exempt under the survivor exemption and the remaining £140,000 to your other chosen beneficiaries, which legacy of £140,000 would also be exempt because it would be below the tax threshold and within the nil rate band of £275,000.

Your widow or surviving civil partner would then have an unmortgaged home (worth £230,000) and £140,000 with the income it produces, in addition to her state bereavement allowance and any private pension, to keep her during her remaining days. On her death £275,000 of her estate of £370,000 would be exempt as not exceeding the tax threshold and the remaining £95,000 would suffer tax at 40 per cent which would amount to £38,000. Thus a tax saving of £56,000 (£94,000 minus £38,000) would have been achieved and would be available to the beneficiaries.

With the high price of homes today a common problem is that for many people the home forms a substantial proportion of the estate. There is insufficient cash or investments which can be left to beneficiaries other than the surviving spouse or partner to make full use of the nil rate band without impoverishing the survivor. Until recently it was thought that a greater tax saving could be achieved if the parties own the house as tenants in common and are prepared for the first to die to use that person's share of the house as part of the £275,000 nil rate band to be left to other beneficiaries (say a daughter) to enable the entirety of the nil rate band to be used. By your will you would leave your one half share of the house and the remaining £140,000 of your estate to your daughter and both bequests would be exempt because your total estate did not exceed the £275,000 tax threshold. Your widow or civil partner would continue to live in the house after your death. On her subsequent death her total estate of £255,000 would similarly not exceed the nil rate band and no tax would be payable on either of the estates, saving £94,000 tax for your daughter to enjoy. Some lawyers now think that for technical reasons this would not now save inheritance tax and the survivor would be considered as having a *right to occupy* the entirety of the property and that its full value would be included in her estate for inheritance tax purposes. We cannot be certain about the inheritance tax saving until the point is tested in court.

The gift would prevent the share left to your daughter being included in the assessment of your civil partner or widow's means should she have to enter a home after your death. If you make lifetime gifts with the intention of depriving yourself of assets which would otherwise be included in the value of your assets used to determine your liability to pay or contribute to residential home fees, the local authority would pursue the donee with a view to including the gift in your assets for that purpose.

To leave the half share of the house to your daughter and not to your spouse or partner would mean that after your death your partner or widow and your daughter would both own and be entitled to use the house. This might not be a good idea, especially if a married daughter were

- to give her share of the house away in the joint lifetime of your survivor or civil partner and the daughter, or
- to predecease your widow or partner intestate or with a will which left her estate to her husband/partner who remarried or entered into a new civil partnership, or to any third party
- or your daughter were to become bankrupt.

Perhaps the solution is not to leave *the share in your home* to your daughter, but to leave her *a legacy equivalent to whichever is the lower of the nil rate band and your share of the home at the date of your death*, the legacy to be charged upon that share. Any such provision would require careful drafting preferably by a professional lawyer.

If your joint estates do not exceed twice the nil rate band, tax can always be completely avoided by equalising the estates and making use of the £275,000 exemption of the nil rate band by leaving the estates to beneficiaries other than the spouse or partner on the first death. If the joint estates exceed twice the tax threshold consider making full use of the lifetime gift exemptions, the nil rate band and the exemption of gifts to spouses and registered civil partners, but in every case take care not to impoverish yourself or your spouse or partner and remember the Inheritance (Provision for Family and Dependants) Act of 1975. Remember also that the survivor exemption only applies to those who are legally married or who have a valid registered civil partnership.

If you do find that you have impoverished yourself or your spouse by making gifts with a view to tax planning there is always the possibility that the donees might be prepared to make a loan repayable on death to the impoverished person, thus assisting during his life but reducing his taxable estate on his death. The loan should be a completely independent arrangement unconnected with, and not a condition or formally tied to, the original gift. Such a loan would also have to be considered carefully from an income tax point of view if a commercial rate of interest were charged, and from the point of view of the gratuitous element being considered as a gift if a commercial rate of interest were not charged.

Equalisation of estates between spouses might also prove to be a wise precaution if a future government were to decide to institute a wealth tax.

The use of survivorship clauses and bequests to your spouse or civil partner

Frequently a provision is put in a will to the effect that any person who does not survive the testator by a stated number of days shall be deemed to have predeceased the testator. The reason for such a clause is to avoid inheritance tax having to be paid for a second time within a short period if the beneficiary dies within a brief period of the testator's death, as may happen if both are involved in a common accident. Great care must be taken when using such a clause if your will contains a bequest to your surviving spouse or civil partner and her financial assets (other than anything she is to inherit from you) are under the tax threshold. The relative size of your estates must be considered. An example will make this clearer.

Suppose that you have an estate of £375,000 and your wife has an estate in her own right of £250,000. You propose to leave £275,000 to your children to make full use of the nil rate band and the remaining £100,000 to your wife if she survives you and to your children if she does not. You include a clause in your will to the effect that any beneficiary who does not survive you for a period of 28 days shall be deemed to have predeceased you. If both you and your wife die in a common accident and she survives you by 20 days, for the purposes of your will, she will be deemed to have predeceased you and your children will inherit your entire estate of £375,000. The first £275,000 of the estate will be exempt because it is within the £275,000 nil rate band and the remaining £100,000 will bear tax at 40 per cent, i.e. £40,000 tax. On your widow's death her estate will be £250,000 and no tax will be payable on her estate because it is below the threshold and within the nil rate band.

If the survivorship clause had not been included, on your death your children would have inherited the £275,000 which would be exempt from tax as not exceeding the threshold and your widow would have inherited the remaining £100,000 of your estate which would be exempt, being a bequest to a surviving spouse. No tax would have been payable on your estate. On your widow's death, the value of her estate including the bequest she inherited from you would be £350,000 and tax of £30,000 (40 per cent of her estate of £350,000 minus the exempt band of £275,000), i.e. 40 per cent of £75,000 would be payable, a saving of £10,000 (£40,000 minus £30,000).

If your wife's estate had been £150,000 and not £250,000 before the accident and the survivorship clause had not been included, on your death no tax would be payable because the £275,000 of your estate left to your children would not exceed the nil rate band and the remainder of your estate would be exempt under the survivor exemption. In addition, on her death her estate of £250,000 (her original £150,000 and the £100,000 she inherited from you) would be exempt from tax because it would not exceed the inheritance tax threshold, a tax saving of £40,000 compared with what would have been the position if the survivorship clause had been included.

In the above examples, for the sake of simplicity I have ignored any lifetime gifts that may have been made, the grossing up rules which are referred to in the next section and assets such as business property in respect of which any tax will be payable at special rates if certain conditions are satisfied.

The case of *Re Figgis* decided in 1969 established several important points in respect of the meaning of words frequently used in survivorship clauses, namely that 'month' prima facie means calendar month and that in computing a period 'from my death' the day of the death is to be excluded and that the time in the day is to be ignored, the full day being included in the computation.

Special rules where exempt beneficiaries are involved

'Grossing up' of legacies and gifts

Reference has been made above to the grossing up of immediately chargeable lifetime gifts. If you do not state that any tax payable in respect of a bequest in your will is to be paid out of the bequest, i.e. that the bequest is subject to tax or to bear its own tax, then unless the property is joint or foreign property, any tax payable will be payable out of the residue of your estate. In these circumstances, if you leave the residue of your estate to an exempt beneficiary such as your spouse or a registered charity, the law directs that, when calculating the inheritance tax payable in respect of your estate, for inheritance tax purposes, any legacies given free of tax shall be 'grossed up', i.e. treated as a legacy of the stated sum and in addition the relevant amount of tax. If you do not remember this point, i.e. that any non-exempt legacy given free of tax is grossed up if the residue of the estate is given to an exempt beneficiary, you could inadvertently exceed the nil rate band with the legacy. You should also bear in mind any non-exempt lifetime gifts you have made when calculating what remains to you of the nil rate band.

The Inland Revenue publish grossing up tables to help you calculate the sums involved, but the easiest way of avoiding trouble in these circumstances is to give the bequests 'subject to tax' and not 'free of tax', or to leave legacies of specific amounts to the exempt beneficiaries and the residue to the non-exempt beneficiaries, to be inherited by them in specified proportions or percentages with a provision that should a residuary beneficiary not be alive or in existence at the date of your death, that beneficiary's interest in your residuary estate shall not lapse but shall accrue to the remaining beneficiaries in the stated proportions.

'Related property' valuation rules

When calculating whether or not a bequest will exceed the nil rate band you must also bear in mind whether or not the Inland Revenue will consider the subject of the bequest to be 'related property'. Related property is property which would have an increased value if owned with other property which is owned by a person or body to whom an exempt transfer could be made, e.g. a spouse or a charity, and whether or not an exempt transfer is or has been made. An example will assist: suppose you own one of a set of three candelabra and your spouse owns the other two, the set of three will be worth more than treble the single candelabra, and even though you may have bought yours at an auction and your spouse inherited hers and even if you propose to leave yours to your son and not to your spouse, the candelabra will be related property for inheritance tax purposes.

Related property is valued in a special way when calculating inheritance tax. To ascertain the inheritance tax valuation of an asset where related property is involved, divide the asset's normal value by the total of its normal value and the normal value of the related property and multiply the result by their combined value. Thus if your candelabra alone is normally worth £100 and your spouse's two candelabra are together worth £300 but the three would be worth £500, then the value of your one candelabra for inheritance tax purposes is £100 divided by (£100 + £300) multiplied by £500, i.e. £100 divided by £400 multiplied by £500, i.e. £0.25 multiplied by £500, i.e. £125.

Cohabitees and the survivor exemption
It is important to remember that in the case of *Holland v IRC*, it was decided that for the purposes of inheritance tax the word 'spouse' only applies to those who are legally married and not to cohabitees, no matter how long the

cohabitees have been living together. The decision does not infringe the right to family life recognised by the European Convention on Human Rights or the Human Rights Act 1998. Long-term partners have been known to marry to obtain the spouse's inheritance tax exemption and widow's bereavement allowance. The Finance Act 2005 has changed the position to the extent that partners in a registered civil partnership have the benefit of the survivor exemption, but it still does not apply to other partners.

Skipping a generation

If your children are wealthy you might wish to consider skipping a generation and instead of leaving bequests to your children, leaving the bequests to or for the benefit of your grandchildren to avoid increased inheritance tax being payable on your children's deaths. In this way the bequest is only taxed once instead of twice before the grandchildren inherit it.

To skip a generation can also have income tax advantages if the grandchildren inherit before they become of age. The income tax advantage arises from the fact that if capital transferred to a child by a parent earns income in excess of £100 in any tax year, the income is taxed as if it were the parent's income, but income earned by capital transferred by a grandparent is treated as the grandchild's own income irrespective of the amount of the income, and if it does not bring the grandchild's income above the grandchild's personal income tax allowance, any income tax deducted from the income can be recovered on behalf of the child.

5

Clauses Recommended to be Included and Clauses Recommended to be Excluded from Your Will

YOUR NAME AND ADDRESS

It might seem simplistic to say so, but besides identifying the document as a will, the will should clearly state whose will it is. The usual way to identify the document as your will is to make sure that it says so by including your name and address but, as in most business matters, carelessness can cause confusion and in legal matters confusion equals expense. The first rule should be to give your true names and all your names, even though you do not normally use some of them or you are usually known by a nickname. Do not shorten a name, e.g. Beth for Elizabeth. If you have assets in a name which is not your true name, include that name as an alias. Thus the first sentence of your will might read, 'This is the last will of me Joseph Anthony Brown otherwise known as Tony Brown of 12 The Street Newtown Essex'. If a parent's names or a child's names are exactly the same as yours, include further identification by describing yourself as Junior or Senior or adding your occupation after your address. In the past, when men followed an occupation for life and women were not generally in employment, it was customary when drafting legal documents that a man should always be described by his occupation and a woman by her legal status such as married woman. Today this might be considered discriminatory.

THE DATE OF THE WILL

Always make certain that your will includes the date upon which it was signed and that codicils include their date and also refer to the date of the will to which they are a codicil. This is a great help if you omit to destroy an earlier will.

A REVOCATION CLAUSE

Include a clause to revoke earlier wills and codicils unless you wish the earlier document to stand as well as the one you are currently making. To avoid confusion, if you wish to make only a few additions or alterations to the earlier will, describe the new document as the first, or second as the case may be, codicil to your will dated [. . .]. If you wish to make numerous alterations it is better to revoke the earlier will and start afresh. It might be more convenient to have more than one subsisting will if each is to relate to property in a different country and they will need to be proved in different countries, but if you do so take care to ensure that the revocation clause in the later will is so worded that it does not inadvertently revoke the earlier will.

THE APPOINTMENT OF EXECUTORS

Chapter 4 has dealt with recommendations as to the number and choice of executors. Suffice it to say here that every will should appoint competent, trustworthy and willing executors who are likely to be available at the appropriate time.

ALTERNATIVE PROVISIONS FOR BEQUESTS TO BENEFICIARIES WHO PREDECEASE YOU AND FOR BEQUESTS THAT FAIL

If you make a bequest to someone and that person dies before you, your will will be treated as though it did not contain the bequest, the bequest will fail and the person's estate will not receive the bequest. In practical terms the effect of the beneficiary dying before you will be that the value of the residue of your estate will be increased by the amount of the bequest unless you include an alternative beneficiary for the gift in your will. If the bequest which fails is a bequest of a share of your residuary estate or of the entire residuary estate, unless you include an alternative beneficiary for the bequest, what is known as a partial intestacy will occur and, although the remainder of your will will take effect, you will be treated as though you have died intestate as far as the bequest is concerned and it will be dealt with according to the intestacy laws.

The same rules apply if a bequest fails for any other reason, for example because the bequest is contrary to the perpetuity law or contrary to public policy.

There are two exceptions to the above rules, namely gifts to charities which show an intention to benefit a charitable cause generally and not just a particular institution, and gifts which come within section 33 of the Wills Act 1837 as amended by the Administration of Justice Act 1982.

Charity is strictly defined for legal purposes and means the relief of poverty, the advancement of education or religion and other purposes beneficial to the community.

In the case of gifts to charity showing a general charitable intention such as a bequest to be used for research into a cure for a disease, if the charitable intention becomes impractical or impossible to carry out (for example once a cure has been found), a court will order that the bequest shall be used for the benefit of other charitable causes as similar as possible to those you intend unless your will shows a contrary intention.

The amended section 33 of the Wills Act provides that if you leave a gift to your child or other descendant such as a grandchild, and the proposed beneficiary dies before you but leaves a descendant who is living at your death, that first-generation descendant of the deceased beneficiary shall receive the bequest and it will not fail, unless your will shows a contrary intention. Illegitimacy is to be disregarded and any child who has been conceived before your death but born alive afterwards is treated as living at your death.

To avoid the complications, uncertainties and unexpected effects which can arise from the above rules it is better, within reason, to include an express provision in your will to provide what shall happen if your beneficiary dies before you. You can do this by stating that the bequest is given 'to X or if he shall die before me to Y' or you might decide to make the bequest 'to such of X, Y and Z as shall survive me and if more than one then equally between them'. Do not use the words 'in equal shares' unless you go on to state what is to happen to the share bequeathed to X, Y or Z if he dies before you. If you wish to leave the bequest to X, Y and Z in unequal shares, include words of accrual such as:

> I devise my farm in Devon as to one half
> thereof to X and as to one quarter thereof to
> each of Y and Z but if X Y or Z shall die
> before me the share of the said farm
> bequeathed to the person who dies before
> me shall not lapse but shall accrue and be
> added to the shares of those who survive me
> and if more than one pro rata so that they
> shall hold the farm in the same relative
> proportions.

Alternative wording could be:

> I devise my farm in Devon to my Trustees
> upon trust to divide the same into four equal
> shares and to hold two of such shares for X a
> further of such shares for Y and the remain-
> ing share for Z provided that if any of the said
> X Y and Z shall die before me the share
> bequeathed to him shall not lapse but shall
> accrue and be added to the other share or
> shares the trusts of which have not failed.

Of course you may take the view that if a beneficiary dies
before you, you will make a codicil or new will, but you
might not have the chance if you lose your testamentary
capacity or otherwise become seriously ill before, or soon
after, your original beneficiary dies.

CLAUSES RELATING TO THE REMARRIAGE OF YOUR SPOUSE OR THE REGISTRATION OF YOUR CIVIL PARTNER'S NEW PARTNERSHIP AFTER YOUR DEATH AND PROVISION FOR CHILDREN OF YOUR PREVIOUS MARRIAGE OR REGISTERED PARTNERSHIP

People are frequently concerned as to what will happen to their assets if they die and leave a spouse who remarries or a partner who enters into a new registered civil partnership after their death. They naturally do not wish their hard earned assets to be inherited via their spouse or partner by someone they have perhaps never even met and they wish to provide for their children as well as their spouse or partner. The problem is compounded by multiple relationships when the testator wishes to provide for the children of an earlier relationship as well as the second spouse or partner and perhaps children of the second relationship. Usually there are too many beneficiaries and not enough estate!

For the sake of easy reading I will write of spouses and marriage but the same points apply in this section to civil partners and registration of civil partnerships.

One possibility which you could consider is to leave your estate to your executors for your spouse during her lifetime or until she shall remarry and thereafter for your children. A problem with such a provision is that your spouse will only be able to spend the income produced by your estate, because if she spends capital, it will not be there to be inherited by the children after her death. Because many of the fixed outgoings which your spouse and yourself have during your joint lives will continue after your death, for example the costs of running your home, the income of your estate will be insufficient to provide a comfortable lifestyle unless it is supplemented by other income of your spouse or unless your estate is a large one.

Further possibilities that might be of assistance in part are

◆ to leave non-income bearing assets to the children;

◆ to leave the matrimonial home to your surviving spouse only during her remaining life;

◆ to leave the matrimonial home to her only during her widowhood; or

◆ to leave your estate to your executors and provide that they shall hold it upon a discretionary trust for your spouse and the children and/or other chosen beneficiaries so that the trustees can make payments from the estate to the trust beneficiaries in the trustees' discretion and according to the beneficiaries' needs as the trustees see them.

If you leave the matrimonial home to your spouse for life, it could cause problems for your spouse's second husband after her death, unless the second husband has his own funds out of which he could buy the home from the children or unless he has an alternative home.

By statute there is now a presumption that makes a gift of property in your will or codicil to your spouse with an interest in the property for your issue ineffective, as far as the gift to your issue is concerned, unless the document shows a contrary intention. Accordingly merely to say 'I give my house to my wife and then to my son' will give your son nothing and it is necessary to say 'I give my house to my wife for the remainder of her life and after her death to my son', or words to that effect.

If you choose to leave the matrimonial home to your spouse for life or only during her widowhood or to set up a discretionary trust, you should ensure that you fully understand the tax implications and it is better to have your will drawn up by a professional who is experienced in tax and in the law of wills.

However you propose to leave your estate, you should always bear in mind the Inheritance (Provision for Family and Dependants) Act 1975 which was referred to in Chapter 3.

MIRROR/MUTUAL WILLS

In Chapter 3 I have written extensively on the subject of mirror wills and mutual wills and I suggest that you refer back to that section and decide whether or not it is appropriate for you to include a declaration in your will as to whether it is a mutual will or a mirror will or whether such a declaration can be safely omitted.

SURVIVORSHIP CLAUSES

In Chapter 4 I have made some observations upon the use of survivorship clauses in wills. Refer back to them to decide whether or not you should include such a clause in your will.

WHO BEARS THE DEBTS, FUNERAL EXPENSES AND EXPENSES INCURRED IN CARRYING OUT YOUR WILL AND INHERITANCE TAX?

Always make sure that you have made it clear in your will from which parts of your estate you intend your debts, funeral expenses and expenses incurred in carrying out your will shall be paid. In Chapter 4 I have dealt with the circumstances in which legacies are grossed up in calculating inheritance tax and I suggest you refer back to that chapter to decide whether your legacies should be given free of tax or subject to tax.

Unless you state otherwise in your will, inheritance tax in respect of lifetime gifts made less than seven years before you die and inheritance tax on joint or foreign property is borne by the person who receives the property or gift and not by those who inherit your residuary estate, but tax on any other kind of property is borne by those who inherit your residuary estate. If you require it to be otherwise you must say so specifically in your will.

GIFTS OF PROPERTY WHICH IS MORTGAGED OR SUBJECT TO A FINANCIAL CHARGE

If you leave property which is mortgaged or security for any other debt such as a local authority charge for unpaid road charges or the cost of keeping a relative in a local authority home, the debt must be paid primarily out of that property unless you show a contrary intention in your will. Merely stating that all your debts are to be paid out of your residuary estate does not in itself show a sufficient contrary intention and you should say that the gift of the property is 'free from all mortgages and all charges subsisting in respect of it at the date of my death'.

GIFTS FOR LIFE

If you leave a building such as your house to someone only for their life, do not forget that you will need to decide who is to be responsible for maintaining the property and paying the outgoings and expenses of occupation such as council tax, water rates and sewage charges, and to set this out in your will. Are such items to be borne by the life tenant or by your residuary estate?

Remember that a life tenant of a property is entitled to live in the property or to have the benefit of the net income produced by the property during their life. Similarly the life tenant of any other trust fund is entitled to the net income produced by the trust fund during their life. If you are thinking of leaving a life interest by your will, consider whether it might be a better idea, in the particular circumstances, to use the principles set out in Chapter 4 in connection with spendthrifts and discretionary trusts and protective trusts instead. You would do this by not leaving the property to the beneficiary for life, but only until the beneficiary dies or goes into a nursing or residential home for the elderly as the beneficiary's normal residence (whichever happens first). This would prevent the income being taken into account by the local authority in assessing contributions to fees. If you decide to do this you will need to consult a professional lawyer for advice and to draft the will.

ADDITIONAL ADMINISTRATIVE POWERS IN WILLS

There are certain powers the general law does not give to your executors but which you can give to them by expressly including a clause in your will to oil the wheels and make their task of carrying out your wishes much easier. Equally there are powers which the general law gives to your executors which you might not wish them to have and which you can expressly exclude by clauses in your will. I will discuss some of these powers below and include specimens of such clauses in the appendix.

Powers of maintenance and advancement in relation to contingent gifts and gifts to minors

If you make a gift to a person which is only to take effect upon the occurrence of a contingency or a gift to a person who is under age, there are statutory and common law powers for your executors to use part of the gift for the maintenance or other benefit of the person concerned before the contingency has been fulfilled or the beneficiary has come of age. The powers are hedged around with complex restrictions and limitations and it is better to give your executors flexibility by including a simpler and wider express clause in your will.

Powers of investment and borrowing

If there is the possibility that the administration of your estate will continue for some time after your death, for example if by your will you leave a life interest or bequests which are contingent upon the happening of some event such as a beneficiary attaining a particular age, you should consider giving your executors wide powers to invest the assets of your estate and to borrow upon them. The powers otherwise given to them by law are limited and cumbersome.

Receipt clauses for bequests to minors and bequests to organisations

Unless you insert a specific clause in your will to authorise it, a minor has no power to give a receipt for a bequest and unless the minor is married or in a registered civil partnership he cannot give a valid receipt for any income it produces. Therefore, if you have left a bequest to a minor, unless you include a suitable receipt clause, your executors will be unable to hand over the bequest until the beneficiary attains his majority; if they do so the beneficiary will be allowed to claim and receive the bequest a second time upon reaching the age of 18 and your executors will have to carry the can.

If you leave a bequest to an organisation such as a charity, it makes life simpler for your executors if you include a clause in your will stating specifically which officers of the organisation can give your executors a valid receipt and discharge for the bequest.

Beneficiaries who cannot be found

Sometimes, in spite of all their best efforts, your executors may not be able to find beneficiaries who are named in your will. Section 27 of the Trustee Act 1925 provides that in such a case your executors shall be free to distribute the estate having regard only to claims of which they have notice after making certain searches and giving 'such notices as would, in any special case, have been directed by a court of competent jurisdiction in an action for administration'. Rather than putting your executors at risk or compelling them to protect themselves by putting your estate to the expense of asking a court what notices it directs should be given, it is better to include in your will a clause setting out a simpler procedure for dealing with the interests of missing beneficiaries.

Limited interests and apportionment of income

If you are leaving a bequest by your will to someone during the beneficiary's lifetime or for a limited period, your executors will find it very helpful if you insert a clause which relieves them of any obligation to apportion, between the beneficiary and those who subsequently become entitled to the bequest, any income which arises from the bequest and straddles the limited and subsequent periods. This is particularly the case if you leave the beneficiary a life interest in the estate and the executors invest the estate in a spread of investments to minimise risk.

Power for executor to carry on a business

A personal representative's power to invest in or carry on a business is hedged around with restrictions and conditions and unless they are complied with it should be wound up and that should be done within one year. If the business is carried on for longer than one year without complying with the restrictions the personal representatives are personally liable for any debts and losses incurred. If you run or are likely to run a business, consider giving your executors power to carry on either alone or in partnership any business in which you are involved as a partner or proprietor at the date of your death and provide that they shall be entitled to be indemnified out of the business for any debts or liabilities reasonably incurred in carrying on the business. A specimen clause can be found in the appendix.

Power for executor to buy property from your estate

An executor has no right to buy property from your estate even though he may offer a good price for it or buy it at auction, unless you authorise him to do so by your will.

Power to appoint new trustees

After your will has been proved your executors can appoint new trustees to act jointly with them in the administration of your estate should that be necessary, but if you wish you can give that power to someone else.

Beneficiaries' power to remove trustees

In essence Section 19 of The Trusts of Land and Appointment of Trustees Act 1996 gives beneficiaries who are together absolutely entitled to trust property and legally competent, power to replace existing trustees with new trustees of the beneficiaries' choice, provided that there is no one still alive who was given power by the will to appoint new trustees. If you do not wish your trustees to have the power to remove the executor trustees you have chosen, exclude the application of this section from your will. The section applies to all trusts unless it is excluded and not just to trusts of land.

The duty of trustees of land to consult with beneficiaries

Section 11(1) of The Trusts of Land and Appointment of Trustees Act 1996 reads 'The trustees of land shall in the exercise of any function relating to land subject to the trust:

(a) so far as is practicable, consult the beneficiaries of full age and beneficially entitled to an interest in possession in the land; and

(b) so far as is consistent with the general interest of the trust, give effect to the wishes of those beneficiaries, or in the case of dispute) of the majority (according to their combined interests).'

This section is vague and uncertain in several respects: what is 'the general interest' of the trust and under what circumstances is it not 'practicable' to consult? Uncertainty leads to disputes and legal disputes are expensive. It is better to exclude the section from the operation of your will. Your trustees do not need statutory authority to authorise them to consult affected beneficiaries before taking major decisions and they are probably always wise to do so in case they are later sued over the decision, whether or not they have a duty to do so. If you trust your trustees, it is better not to fetter their powers. If you do not trust them, appoint someone else instead.

The extent of liability for acts done in the administration of your estate

You might wish to consider including a clause in your will to exempt non-professional executors from legal liability for their acts and omissions in the administration of your estate unless the acts constitute fraud or gross negligence. Without such a clause such executors, who are unlikely to be insured against negligence in the performance of executorship duties, might well be unwilling to accept the position. Everyone makes mistakes from time to time. Such a clause will not be void on the grounds of public policy, even if the executor drew up the will for you.

Attestation clause

Your will should always include what is known as an attestation clause, i.e. a clause which explains the circumstances in which it was signed and witnessed to show that they comply with the requirements of the Wills Act.

Settling old scores

Finally, do not attempt to settle old scores by your will. The probate document will omit anything which is libellous or blasphemous.

6

Points on Which You Should Take Special Care When Drafting Your Will

Do not use phrases such as 'I hope that', 'I trust that', or 'I request'; be definite if you intend your wishes to be carried out.

Be precise and avoid vague wording which will make gifts fail to take effect by reason of a lack of certainty. It is much safer to take care and state your intentions unambiguously rather than rely upon someone attempting to guess them. The devil himself knoweth not the mind of man – or of woman either if it comes to that!

The courts will lean over backwards to give effect to your intentions but they will not make your will for you. Courts have very limited powers to look beyond the wording of your will to ascertain your intention. They are only permitted to do so if the wording of the will is meaningless or shown to be ambiguous on the face of the will or in the light of surrounding circumstances. If this is not so and the wording of your will appears to show your intentions clearly, the courts have no power to hear evidence as to what you actually intended and must give effect to your wishes *as expressed* in your will, even though external evidence would have shown that the wording of your will did not express your wishes correctly.

If your intention in any part of your will is not clear after taking into account any external evidence it is permitted to consider, a court must ignore that part of the will and it will not take effect. You must therefore make your meaning absolutely clear and unambiguous at all times. It is so easy to think, incorrectly, that because you know what you mean, that is what you have written and it is a good idea to have someone read over your will for you to see if they are clear about what you intend and to check that what they think you intend is in fact what you intend. If you do not make it clear what you intend to give and whom you intend shall benefit from the gift, the gift may well fail to take effect completely by reason of uncertainty.

If a court is satisfied, after considering the evidence it is permitted to consider, that the wording of your will does not carry out your intentions because of a clerical error or the failure of the draftsman (if it was prepared for you by someone else) to understand the intentions, it can rectify your will so as to carry out your intentions. Although a court can interpret the meaning of the words of your will, it cannot rectify the wording of your will for any other reason.

A striking example of the lengths to which a court will go to use its power to rectify a will to achieve a testator's intention is the case of Vautier's Estate. The facts were that a husband and wife signed each other's wills by mistake, the wills having been prepared in reciprocal terms. The mistake did not come to light until after the wife's death.

The court decided that the will she had not signed could not be proved as her will, because she had not signed it and completed it in accordance with the required formalities. However, the will she had signed would be rectified to carry out her perceived intention and was allowed to be proved as her will after the wording had been amended. Although this was a Jersey case it is thought that the result would be the same in England or Wales.

IDENTIFICATION OF BENEFICIARIES

Describe beneficiaries by their full correct names rather than merely using their relationship to you, and give their addresses. This will be of assistance to your executors, not only in identifying the beneficiaries, but also in tracing them. If this is not possible because you intend to benefit a fluctuating group of people identified by description, such as your nephews, specify a cut-off date. Take care to say whether you intend to include only members of that group who are living at the date of your will or also those born after the date of your will and before your death. Any person conceived but not born at the date of your death is considered to be living. If you wish to include members of a group who are born after your death, remember that it will not be possible to distribute your bequest until it is no longer possible for anyone else to join the group covered by the description.

Remember also the complicated rules of the Perpetuity and Accumulations Act 1964 (dealt with in more detail later in this chapter) and that in case the Act should invalidate the bequest, it is safer not to make any gift by your will in respect of which gift all the beneficiaries will not have been ascertained and qualified for their share of the bequest within 21 years of your death.

If you leave a bequest to relatives by the description of their relationship to you, such as nieces, nephews, uncles or aunts, make it clear whether you intend to include only blood relatives or whether you intend to include relatives by marriage, (e.g. the daughters of your wife's sister as your nieces) and by civil partnership registration.

A gift to your 'issue' or 'descendants' will mean that each of such people who are living at the date of your death will inherit an equal share. If this is not what you intend and your intention is that any such person shall inherit only if their ancestors who are your descendants have all died before you, make your gift to your 'descendants per stirpes'. (Please refer to the explanations of 'Gifts per stirpes' and 'Gifts per capita' in the glossary.)

A gift to your children will be taken to include your adopted and your illegitimate children (if any), but not your stepchildren unless you indicate in your will that that is not your intention or you have no other children at the date of the will, but any person who has been treated as a child of your family in respect of your marriage, your former marriage or registered civil partnership will have a right to make a claim for reasonable provision from your estate under the Inheritance (Provision for Family and Dependants) Act 1975, as amended.

The words 'relations' or 'next of kin' will usually be taken to mean those who will inherit your estate if you die intestate. (Please refer to Chapter 1.)

Do not use nicknames. A bequest to 'mother' led to litigation where a testator was in the habit of calling his wife 'mother' and both the wife and natural mother were living at his death.

If you make a gift to charity, identify it by its exact name and registered number and say that the gift is made for its charitable purposes. In a case in which the charity was in the course of liquidation at the date of the testator's death and the will did not say that the gift is made for its charitable purposes, the court decided that the gift took effect for the benefit of the charity's creditors and did not have the benefit of inheritance tax relief because the creditors were not a charitable purpose.

The registered number of a charity can be obtained directly from the charity or from the Charity Commission of Harmsworth House, 13–15 Bouverie Street, London EC4Y 8DP. Tel: 0870 333 0123. Website: www.charity-commission.gov.uk.

To understand what will happen to any bequest to a beneficiary who dies before you or a bequest which fails to take effect for any other reason, if you have made no alternative provision in your will, please refer to the section in Chapter 5 headed 'Alternative provisions for bequests to beneficiaries who predecease you and for bequests that fail'.

DESCRIPTION OF BEQUESTS

In the same way as it is necessary to be precise when describing beneficiaries it is necessary to avoid uncertainty when describing what you intend to give.

Do not use vague phrases such as 'a substantial legacy', 'fair recompense', 'some of my'.

If you have several items that fit a description, e.g. several tea services, do not say merely 'my tea service'; rather particularise the item further by saying, for example, 'my Royal Doulton carnation patterned tea service'.

It is not a good idea to include a large number of bequests of individual items in your will: you might not own them at your death and your beneficiaries might feel embarrassed to decline or discard them but not really want them. If you give a legacy of, say, a car, make it clear as to whether the legacy refers to the car you own now or to any car you might own at the date of your death.

Similarly it is not a good idea to leave a particular bank or building society account or the money in such an account as a bequest; the balance in the account at any particular time will vary and when you die at some (hopefully) long time in the future, the account might have been closed.

Describe property by its postal address 'and the land and premises occupied therewith'.

Make it clear whether any bequest you make is given 'subject to tax', in which case the beneficiary bears any inheritance tax payable in respect of it, or 'free of tax', in which case the tax is payable by your residuary estate. In the absence of any provision to the contrary in your will, tax in respect of joint or foreign property will be borne by the beneficiary but tax in respect of other property will be borne by your residuary estate.

If you wish to leave a bequest to your executor or to someone who is a trustee under your will for their own benefit, state that the bequest is given to them 'absolutely'.

A bequest of something which you do not own at the date of your death will not take effect except in the special circumstances of the doctrine of election discussed in Chapter 3 under the heading 'Other property you do not own over which you have no power of appointment'.

Bequeathing something by your will does not prevent you from subsequently disposing of it later in your lifetime to the beneficiary or to any other person.

LEGACIES TO THOSE WHO OWE YOU MONEY AND TO THOSE TO WHOM YOU OWE MONEY

If you leave a bequest to someone who owes you money, make it clear in your will as to whether you intend that the legacy shall be paid and the debt forgiven or whether the debt shall be deducted from the legacy.

If you leave a legacy to a creditor, make it clear whether you intend the legacy to be in substitution for or in addition to the debt.

THE MEANING OF SOME WORDS AND PHRASES

Do not attempt to use technical terms in your will if ordinary words will do.

In order to achieve your intentions as expressed in your will, the courts will interpret words according to the context in which you use them, but it can be useful to know how they have been interpreted in the past.

The words 'family' and 'my relations' have been variously interpreted and if possible it is better not to use these words.

'Next of kin': the phrase 'next of kin' is interpreted in accordance with the order set out for inheritance on intestacy (see Chapter 1).

'My money' has been variously interpreted according to its context in the will as a whole and might be taken as referring only to cash, or on the other hand to include bank accounts or investments: it is better not to use the term without further amplification.

'My personal estate', 'my personal effects', 'my goods and chattels' or 'my belongings' are usually taken to include all your moveable items, but not your freehold or leasehold property. However, 'my estate' or 'my possessions' is usually construed as meaning all your assets including non-moveable property.

'Personal' estate or 'personal' chattels will not usually be construed to include items used for business purposes.

A useful and comprehensive, if somewhat dated, definition of personal chattels can be found in section 55 (1) (x) of the Administration of Estates Act 1925:

> 'Personal chattels' mean carriages, horses, stable furniture and effects (not used for

business purposes), motor cars and accessories (not used for business purposes), garden effects, domestic animals, plate, plated articles, linen, china, glass, books, pictures, prints, furniture, jewellery, articles of household or personal use or ornament, musical and scientific instruments and apparatus, wines, liquors and consumable stores, but do not include any chattels used at the death ... for business purposes nor money or securities for money.

This definition can be incorporated in your will if you wish by providing 'I bequeath my personal chattels as defined by section 55(1)(x) of the Administration of Estates Act 1925 to ...'.

'Month' means calendar month unless lunar month or four weeks is specifically stated.

'From' a date does not include the date.

However, I repeat that the meaning of the words you use will always be decided according to the context in which they are used looking at the will as a whole.

VOID PROVISIONS IN WILLS

Earlier in this chapter I explained that an attempted bequest will fail if the subject of the bequest or the beneficiary to whom it is given is not described in such a way that it is certain. Your bequest may also fail because it falls within the following kinds of gifts:

Gifts to those who witness your will

You need only two witnesses to the signing of your will or codicil, but if you leave a bequest to one of the witnesses or to the spouse or civil partner of one of the witnesses, although the choice of witness will not invalidate your will, the choice of witness will invalidate the bequest and it will not take effect unless the witness's signature can be regarded as superfluous because you have used two other disinterested witnesses. To avoid problems do not choose beneficiaries or the spouses or civil partner of beneficiaries as witnesses to your signature.

Gifts which are contrary to law or contrary to public policy

If you include a bequest in your will which the law considers to be contrary to law or public policy, the gift will not achieve your wishes. If the bequest is considered to be essentially evil, e.g. a bequest conditional upon murdering someone, the bequest will fail completely, but if the condition upon which the bequest is given is merely prohibited by law or public policy, the condition will be void. If you intend that the gift shall only take effect if the condition is fulfilled, i.e. the condition is what is known as a *condition precedent* and the condition is void, the gift will fail completely, but if you intended that the gift shall take effect but cease if the condition is fulfilled, i.e. the condition is what is known as a *condition subsequent*, the gift will take effect free from the void condition. An example of a gift with a condition precedent is a gift to your son if he successfully completes the university course he is taking and an example of a condition subsequent is a gift to him, but if he fails the course, then to your daughter, although both of these conditions are of course valid ones.

You must distinguish between conditions (which may or may not be valid) and limitations which are restrictions upon the period of ownership, i.e. gifts until an event occurs, which are always valid.

Exactly what is considered to be contrary to public policy changes from time to time but a few principles can be stated.

♦ Gifts that weaken the family unit or the institution of marriage are contrary to public policy. Therefore if you leave a gift to your son if he leaves his wife the gift will not take effect because it is a condition which is void being both contrary to public policy and a condition precedent.

♦ Conditions contrary to the inherent legal nature of property, e.g. that it shall not be sold or shall be boarded up and not used for a long specified time, are contrary to public policy.

♦ Conditions which interfere with the right of a parent to control the education or religious upbringing of his child are contrary to public policy.

If you provide in your will that a bequest is to be forfeited if the beneficiary challenges the will, such a provision is not considered to be contrary to public policy, but the bequest might fail to take effect for reasons of uncertainty, unless it is carefully drafted.

Gifts which infringe the rules against perpetuities and accumulations

The law contains very complex rules which are mainly contained in the Perpetuities and Accumulations Act 1964, which prevent the income from a bequest being accumulated and added to the capital of the bequest by the personal representatives for an excessive period, rather than distributed to the beneficiary, and which prevent bequests being made to beneficiaries whose identity might not be ascertained for an excessively long time in the future. These rules are known as the rules against perpetuities and accumulations. If you wish to make a bequest and the identity of the beneficiary might not be ascertained within 21 years of your death, e.g. a gift 'to my grandchildren whether born before or after my death', be sure to consult a solicitor about the wording and to check whether it can be legally done. Similarly, if you wish the income of a bequest to be accumulated for a period that could exceed 21 years, consult a solicitor.

SECTION 33 OF THE WILLS ACT 1837, AS AMENDED

By this section, if you leave a gift to a descendant and that beneficiary dies before you but leaves his descendant who is living at your death, the bequest will take effect as a bequest to the descendant who is living at your death, unless your will shows a contrary intention. If it is not your intention that the bequest shall be construed in this way make your intention clear, for example by stating expressly what is to happen to the bequest if your nominated beneficiary predeceases you.

THE EFFECT OF DIVORCE OR ANNULMENT OF YOUR MARRIAGE OR DISSOLUTION OF YOUR CIVIL PARTNERSHIP ON YOUR WILL

Effect on bequests to your spouse

Dissolution of your marriage or civil partnership does not invalidate your will, but a decree absolute (not a decree nisi) makes any bequest in the will to your spouse or civil partner as the case may be take effect as if the former spouse or partner had died on the date the decree becomes absolute, leaving bequests in the remainder of your will valid. Usually the bequest will become part of the residue of your estate and go to your residuary beneficiaries, but if the bequest is of the entire estate or of a share of the residue of the estate, it will be treated as not having been disposed of by your will and will be inherited on your death according to the laws of intestacy.

Effect on spouse's or partner's power of appointment, executorship and trusteeship

Similarly, any provisions in your will conferring powers of appointment on your spouse or partner (i.e. power for him to appoint or choose a beneficiary for part of an estate) or appointing him as an executor or trustee take effect after a decree absolute of dissolution of your marriage or civil partnership as if the former spouse or partner had died on the date the decree became absolute.

Effect on your spouse or partner as guardian

Unless a contrary intention is apparent from your will, an appointment of your spouse or civil partner as a guardian of an under-age child is revoked by a decree of divorce, annulment or dissolution which either is made in a court in England or Wales or would be recognised by such a court.

Because the above effects only occur on a decree absolute, take care to make a new will as soon as it is clear that your partnership or marriage has irretrievably broken down, because if you die before decree absolute, any will you have will stand and if you merely revoke your will, your estate will be distributed as though you were intestate.

(7)

The International Element of Wills

In these days of easy travel, holidays abroad, comparative affluence, early retirement, armed conflicts and the globalisation of business, it is becoming increasingly common for people to own property, work and retire in countries other than those in which they were born. In these circumstances, consideration of how foreign factors can affect your will is becoming increasingly important.

FORMALITIES FOR COMPLETION OF A VALID WILL IF YOU ARE OUTSIDE ENGLAND AND WALES

The formalities that have to be followed to make a valid will if you are in England or Wales have been dealt with in Chapter 2. If you make a will without observing those formalities while you are abroad, English law will accept it as validly made if it is made

- in accordance with the formalities required by the state where it was made; or

- in accordance with the formalities required by the state where at the time the will was made or at your death you were domiciled or had your habitual residence or of which you were a national.

If the will deals with immoveable property such as a holiday villa, it will also be recognised as valid by English law as regards that property if it complies with the formalities required by the law of the state in which the property is situated.

If you make your will on a ship or aircraft the will will also be treated as validly completed if its completion conforms to the law of the country with which the ship or aircraft has the closest connection.

An alternative provision to validate wills made abroad was provided by the Convention providing for a Uniform Law on the Form of an International Will. The provisions of this convention will be incorporated into English law by the section 28 of the Administration of Justice Act 1982 when the section is brought into force by a commencement order. Unfortunately, although the convention has been adopted by parts of Canada, by Ecuador, Libya, Niger, Portugal and the former Yugoslavia, and the Act was passed over 20 years ago, no commencement order appears to have been made. As mentioned in Chapter 1, such matters do not rank highly upon the political agenda.

For your will to be valid under the convention:

◆ The will must be made in writing.

◆ You must declare in front of an 'authorised person' and two other witnesses that the document is your will and that you are aware of its contents and you must sign the will at the end of the will or acknowledge your signature, in either case, in their presence.

- The authorised person and the witnesses must immediately sign at the end of the will in your presence to attest it.

- If the will consists of more than one page, each page must be numbered and signed by the authorised person and yourself.

- The authorised person must prepare a certificate in the prescribed form to the effect that the formalities have been complied with.

WILLS RELATING TO PROPERTY WHICH IS SITUATED OUTSIDE OF ENGLAND AND WALES

The previous section dealt with the formalities to be followed when making a will abroad if it is to be recognised as valid in English law, but in considering any property you may have which is situated abroad, you must also consider the foreign law relating to the property and the making of wills, even if the will is made in the United Kingdom. Some states have restrictions in relation to who can inherit property and the tax laws relating to property differ from those of English law. The procedure and formalities for making a will that is to be recognised by the foreign country as a valid document of title to the property are usually different from those of England and Wales. It is usually better to make a will in the country where the property is situated to deal with foreign property, or at least to obtain advice from a lawyer who practises in the law of the relevant country.

You can have several valid wills at the same time and separate wills dealing with different parts of your estate, e.g. a will covering your English property and a separate will covering your foreign property. If you do so, make sure that the foreign will does not contain a clause revoking your English will or any codicil, and similarly make sure that your English documents do not revoke the foreign will. A clause in the later will such as 'I revoke all wills and testamentary documents previously made by me' would revoke the other will. Take care in each will to make it clear that the English property/the foreign property/the will, as appropriate, is excluded from the revocation clause.

8

Revoking or Amending Your Will

AMENDING YOUR WILL

If you make an error when you are typing or writing out your will, it is better to destroy it and start again, but if you decide that to do so would be too inconvenient, you can cross out the offending word or words or, if appropriate make an interlineation or insertion, but whatever you decide to do make sure that after the alteration the will remains legible and your meaning is clear and unambiguous. All alterations must be initialled, first by you and then by those who witness your signature and before the final signing process is completed, to show that the alterations were made *before* the will was completed. If the alterations are not initialled in this way and the original writing is still legible, a court will give effect to the will in its unaltered form, but if the alterations are not initialled and the original wording has been obliterated and is illegible, both the original and the altered wording will be ignored and the will will take effect as there is a blank space in the will.

If you decide that you wish to change your will after you have made it, ideally you should revoke the will and make a new will, but if the changes are minor, such as deleting or adding a beneficiary, guardian or executor, you can do so by making a codicil to your will. A codicil is a separate supplementary document which adds to or varies an existing testamentary document; a specimen form of codicil is to be found in the appendix to this book. If you do make a codicil, be certain to read it over in conjunction with the will and any codicils you may have made earlier to be sure that the provisions of the documents do not conflict. Codicils must be signed and witnessed in accordance with the rules set out in Chapter 2 for the signing of wills, but your will and its codicils need not have the same witnesses.

REVOKING YOUR WILL

The privileged wills of those engaged in actual military service and sailors at sea

In the same way as you can make a will at any age and orally or without any formalities if you are one of the above persons, you can similarly revoke your will at any age and orally or without any formalities if you come within the above classes.

If you do not come within one of the above classes your will will only be revoked in one of the following ways.

Revocation by marriage or registration of a civil partnership

With the exception of what is said below in respect of the exercise of a power of appointment by will if you have an existing will when you enter into a valid marriage or civil partnership, the mere fact of the marriage or partnership will revoke the will unless the will states that it was made with that particular marriage or partnership in mind and you do not intend it to revoke the will. The will may show your intention in respect of the person concerned either by expressly saying so or by clear implication, such as referring to him as your fiancée or future husband or partner.

If you wish the will to be effective only if the event takes place, say in the will that it is to be conditional upon it taking place within a specified period, for example, a year. If a will apparently made with a particular marriage or partnership registration in mind is not made conditional upon the marriage or partnership registration taking place within a specified period it will be effective until it is revoked by one or more of the other methods of revoking wills.

Marriage to or registration of a partnership with one person will, of course, revoke a will which states that it is made in contemplation of marriage or partnership with a different person.

Any appointment of property which you make by your will in the exercise of a power of appointment which you have will not be revoked by you subsequently registering a civil partnership unless the property would form part of your estate if you had not made the appointment.

Revocation by destroying the will with the intention to revoke it

Your will will be revoked if it is destroyed by you or by another person at your request and in your presence. In either case you must intend that the will shall be revoked.

The formalities must be strictly followed and you must have the requisite intention. It is not sufficient to write 'revoked' on the will or to cross out part of the will. If the will is only partially destroyed or obliterated, e.g. by tearing a piece out of the will, unless that piece is a vital part of the will, only the part torn out or obliterated will be revoked and the rest of the will will remain valid. Neither is it sufficient if you accidentally destroy the will or if you are so drunk that you do not know what you are doing when you do it or you otherwise lack mental capacity. Moreover, if you ask someone to destroy your will for you, the destruction will be ineffective unless it is done in your presence: for this purpose presence is narrowly interpreted and it is not sufficient if they take it into another room to destroy it.

Implied revocation

If you make a later will or codicil containing no revocation clause but containing provisions which are inconsistent with your earlier will, the provisions of your earlier will which are inconsistent with the later one will be considered to be revoked, but the other provisions of the earlier will will remain valid, as will all the provisions of the later will.

If you make a later will or codicil containing no revocation clause and the provsions are not inconsistent with your earlier will, both the earlier will and the later document will be effective.

Express revocation

By far the best way of revoking provisions of your will is

to make a new will or codicil which contains a clause to revoke the earlier will in its entirety or to revoke only the provisions which you wish to revoke. If you have several wills, for example a will dealing with your property in England and another will dealing with property abroad, take great care to ensure that the revocation clause revokes only the will that you intend to revoke and that you do not unintentionally revoke both wills.

Dependent relative revocation

For the sake of completeness I mention that if you purport to revoke a will or a bequest on the basis that a new will or bequest which you make is valid, or that the old bequest is covered by the laws of intestacy and this is not so, then the old will or bequest will stand and not be revoked. This rule is known in law as the doctrine of dependent relative revocation. An example is the recent case of *Re Finnemore (Deceased)* in which the testatrix had made three wills each of which contained revocation clauses and benefited her daughter. The daughter's husband witnessed the last two wills and this would normally caused the bequests to the daughter to fail. However, the court decided that the revocation clauses in the later wills were intended to be conditional upon the gifts to the daughter in those wills taking effect and because the gifts in those wills were made void by the husband witnessing the wills, the bequest to the daughter in the first will would not be revoked and would take effect.

9

General Advice Concerning Wills and Associated Matters

THE SAFEKEEPING OF YOUR WILL

Your will will be of no use whatsoever if it cannot be found after your death, so make sure that it is kept safely and that your family and your executors know where it is kept. You can also register the whereabouts of your will on the internet website www.lst.locate.co.uk There is no charge for this service which merely notes that you have made a will and where it is to be found. It does not note what the contents of the will are.

If the will is made by a solicitor, he will usually be prepared to keep it in safe custody for you and supply you with a copy free of charge, in the hope that your executors will entrust him with the probate work at the relevant time. Your bank will also be prepared to keep your will in safe custody, but will almost certainly charge an annual fee. If you wish you can deposit your will with the Probate Registry during your lifetime for safe custody at a nominal charge. The fee at the time of writing is £15 and the cheque for the fee should be made payable to HM Paymaster General. For details of the procedure and the special envelope in which the documents must be deposited, telephone the Record Keeper's Department of The Principal Probate Registry (020 7947 7000) or write to the department at Principal Probate Registry, 1st Avenue House, 42–49 High Holborn, London WC1V 6NP. The documents are deposited in a sealed envelope and can be deposited in person by you or by someone on your behalf with your authority, at any probate registry or sent by post for deposit to the above address only. If your will is deposited with the Registry it will give you a certificate of deposit which you must keep safely because the certificate will have to be produced if your will is to be produced or withdrawn. There is no fee payable if you wish to withdraw your will from deposit. Depositing your will with the Registry ensures that unscrupulous persons cannot tamper with it after your death. The Registry keeps an index of wills which is searched every time anyone seeks to take out a grant of representation to an estate and thus ensures that your will will not be overlooked and that no earlier will which you may have made, but not destroyed, is proved by mistake. A further possibility is to keep your will in a safe place at home with your other business papers, but if possible make sure it is kept in a fireproof place. Wherever your will is kept it is a good idea to make sure that there is a copy of the will in existence and the copy is kept elsewhere and clearly marked 'copy', because it is sometimes possible to prove a copy will if the original is accidentally destroyed or lost.

To prove your will if it has been lost there must be reasonable evidence both that the will was properly made and what its contents were. As Lord Justice Jacobs said in the case of *Parks v Clout in 2003*, the formalities set out in the Wills Act 'do really matter. One must have a reasonably firm basis for concluding that the formalities were carried out, not merely what the substance of the will was.' Hearsay evidence is admissable to prove the existence or otherwise of the will and the existence and contents of a will can be proved by circumstantial evidence, but there must still be reasonable evidence of both the existence of the will and what its contents were. It must be proved on a balance of probabilities that the will, in those terms, was completed in accordance with the formal requirements of the Wills Act and the burden of proof is upon the person who seeks to uphold the document as a valid will. A higher standard of proof is required to prove fraudulent behaviour such as fraudulent destruction of your will.

Your will or the copy should always be easily accessible to you to refresh your memory on the occasions when you may wish to consider revising it, although you may not wish to consider revising it as frequently as a former Lord Chancellor, Lord St Leonards. He made eight codicils to his will and made his daughter read it through to him so frequently that when the will could not be found after his death, she was able to satisfy a court that she could recite it verbatim!

INFORMATION FOR YOUR EXECUTORS

To assist those you leave behind, create a file or computer disk of the information your executors and family are likely to need at your death and when dealing with your will and winding up your estate. Your family and executors will need to register your death, prove your will and administer your estate and you will not be around to supply information or to tell them where documents can be found! Do not forget to make them aware of the existence of the file and where you keep it.

The file should include the following:

- A detailed note of any special funeral wishes. These could include your choice of a preferred funeral director and your request as to the disposal and treatment of the body or of the ashes if there is to be a cremation. A preference could be expressed for a religious or humanist funeral, for special readings or music, for flowers or donations to favoured charities in lieu. Alternatively you could leave these matters to the family's discretion. Give details of any prepaid funeral plans and the deeds of burial rights you may have for a grave.

- A notification list of the names, addresses and contact details of all those you wish to be notified of your death.

- A note of the whereabouts of your will, birth, civil partnership and marriage certificates, national insurance number, any decree of dissolution of marriage or partnership, pension documents, benefits books or papers. The information in these documents will be required to register your death.

- Prepare an assets and liabilities schedule and documents locator to assist your executors when they come to prove your will and settle up your financial affairs. This should include a list of your assets such as bank and building society accounts, National Savings investments, shareholdings and life assurance policies and details of any debts such as personal loans and mortgages. Remember to include a note of where relevant documents such as motor vehicle documents, share or stock certificates, building society pass books, property title deeds, insurance policies documents (including house, contents, life and motor policies), hire, hire-purchase, credit sale and rental agreements can be found and contact details including account numbers (but not security numbers) and addresses. Include your income tax details and details of pensions, credit and debit cards, particulars of any guarantees of any mortgages or other debts you have given, the names and addresses of your accountants and solicitors, the dates and amounts of any gifts you have made which are not exempt from inheritance tax and the identity and addresses of the beneficiaries.

LIVING WILLS AND ADVANCE DIRECTIVES

Your will is a document which declares your intention as to what is to take place on or after your death and usually, but not necessarily, deals with the disposal of your property. A living will is not a will in the true sense of the word. A living will is the popular name for what lawyers call an advance directive, that is to say a document which sets out what medical treatment you wish, or do not wish, to undergo in specified circumstances before your death.

Advance directives are recognised by the common law and have their origin in the fact that, as one judge has put it, 'a mentally competent patient has an absolute right to consent or refuse consent to medical treatment for any reason, rational or irrational, or for no reason at all even where that decision may lead to his or her own death'. The question is one of your right to self-determination and what you see to be in your best interest. For others, such as doctors, to override your wishes is 'benevolent paternalism' and a criminal and civil assault. Medical treatment must not be confused with basic nursing care. There is no right to refuse basic nursing care essential to keep you as comfortable as possible such as washing and feeding by spoon as opposed to artificial feeding.

To have a right to forgo medical treatment or have it withdrawn at your request is not the same thing as having a right to die, even if death will inevitably follow. The European Court has confirmed in the case of *Pretty v United Kingdom* that there is no general right to die as such in English law. If you are mentally competent but physically incapable, a general right to die would involve the assistance of others in the withdrawal of basic medical care or the introduction of a positive element with the primary intention of causing death, both of which are unlawful euthanasia. Although a bill entitled the 'Assisted Dying for the Terminally Ill Bill' has been presented to Parliament to allow a competent adult, who is suffering unbearably from a terminal or serious and progressive illness, to receive medical help to die at his own considered and persistent request and to cover the provision of pain relief medication for a person suffering from such an illness, it has not yet been – and may never be – passed.

Advance directives are useful in that they may be relied upon if at a future date you lose the powers of making decisions or communication, e.g. as a result of falling into a coma or suffering a stroke. They can save relatives and doctors much worry about what you would wish when agonising decisions have to be made and help them to achieve the correct decision.

There is as yet no Act of Parliament governing living wills in English law, although the Mental Capacity Bill which is now being considered by Parliament contains proposals to put them on a statutory footing and sets out the formalities which will be necessary to make them valid. Unless and until the bill is passed there are no set formalities for advance directives, but common law principles suggest that to be valid your living will must be freely made and you must be mentally capable of making balanced judgements and at least 18 years old at the time the will is made. The will must state your true wishes and accordingly it must be made voluntarily, without pressure, influence or encouragement by any other person. Your judgement must not be adversely affected by illness, mental upset or anything else when you make the will.

The advance directive should clearly state the nature of the treatment you wish to have or to refuse and the circumstances in which it is to be acted upon. The directive should make it clear that you understand both the treatment and its likely effect.

The will must not have been revoked, even orally, by the time the question of carrying out the treatment arises and if tested in a court, the court will take into account, but not necessarily follow, your orally expressed wishes, even if you are under the age of 18. To assist from an evidential point of view if it comes to be tested in court, an advance directive should be in writing, dated and signed and witnessed by at least one independent witness who will have nothing to gain from your death.

Discussing the will with the family members could lead to the suggestion that they may have applied undue influence.

If you make a living will you should review it frequently because your wishes may change in the light of advances in medical science and care should be taken to ensure that you make the existence of the will and any changes to it known to your doctor, e.g. by lodging it with him. You should also consider and enquire of the relevant company whether it would consider any life or endowment policy you might have might be invalidated by the will on the grounds that you might be considered to have committed suicide.

ENDURING POWERS OF ATTORNEY

In the same way as your will makes provision for your wishes to be carried out when you are no longer alive, an Enduring Power of Attorney is a useful tool to appoint someone you trust and have confidence in to act for you if you become incapable of acting for yourself during your lifetime. With average life expectancy increasing such situations are arising more frequently. Most lawyers consider that it is almost as important for you to set up an Enduring Power of Attorney as it is to make a will and that wills and Enduring Powers of Attorney complement each other.

A Power of Attorney is a document by which a person (the donor) gives to one or more people he or she chooses (the attorney(s)) power to deal with some specified financial affairs and property of the donor or the donor's affairs and property generally.

Before 1985, powers automatically became ineffective if you became mentally incapable and it was necessary for an application to be made to the Court of Protection to appoint a Receiver to manage your financial matters for you under the court's supervision. Receivership applications are onerous, lengthy and very expensive. In 1985 Parliament passed the Enduring Powers of Attorney Act which created a new, simple form of power of attorney called an Enduring Power of Attorney which will survive any mental incapacity you might suffer, provided that (a) you are over the age of 18 and mentally capable when you sign it, (b) you are not an undischarged bankrupt, (c) you use the prescribed form of document and (d) that you follow the procedures set up by the Act. The latest form of Enduring Power of Attorney can be downloaded from the Stationery Office website at www.hmso.gov.uk or purchased from a law stationer. The form contains notes on how to complete it.

You must sign the form (or it must be signed on your behalf if you are unable to sign) in the presence of an independent witness, i.e. someone other than the attorney and preferably someone other than your spouse. After the form has been so signed the witness must also sign the form and if the form is signed on your behalf, two independent witnesses are required. The attorney or, if there are more than one attorney, each attorney has a separate part of the form to complete and to sign and the signatures of the attorney(s) must be similarly witnessed before you become mentally incapable if the Enduring Power of Attorney is to have legal effect. An attorney cannot witness the signature of another attorney or that of the donor.

If more than one person is appointed attorney the form can be completed to appoint them to act jointly, in which case one cannot act without the other and if one refuses the appointment, dies, or becomes bankrupt or otherwise incapable of acting the power will become ineffective. Alternatively the attorneys may be appointed to act jointly and severally, in which case either has power to act alone and the power remains effective as long as there is one attorney who is capable of acting and willing to act.

It is possible to limit the attorney(s) powers by inserting in the form restrictions, for example, as to what the power covers or stating that in certain specified transactions the consent of one or more third parties is required or in the case of joint and several attorneys, that they must all join in. Thus the form can state the power shall not come into effect until you become incapable, that it shall be limited to managing investments, that all cheques over a specified sum require two signatures or that a property cannot be sold without the agreement of your spouse or all your children.

When the power of attorney is in force, unless the Enduring Power of Attorney places limits on the attorney's powers, the attorney can do almost anything you could have done, for example the attorney can sell your shares or other property, use your bank account and make birthday, wedding anniversary and Christmas presents from your property of a reasonable amount to those connected with you (even to the attorney). An attorney cannot be appointed to act in matters of personal status such as adoption, marriage or divorce or given power to appoint anyone to act in his stead or as his successor. Neither can an attorney make a will for you, but he can ask the Court of Protection (of which the Public Guardianship Office is the administrative arm) to make a will for you if that is in your interest. If you wish to delegate powers which you have as a trustee, a solicitor should be consulted because the law concerning a trustee's power to delegate is complicated. Your attorney cannot decide matters relating to your medical care, but this may well be changed if the Mental Capacity Bill, which is at present (2005) before parliament and which seeks to abolish Enduring Powers of Attorney and replace them by 'Lasting Powers of Attorney', becomes law.

You can give separate Enduring Powers of Attorney to different attorneys in respect of different assets or matters. If both you and your wife wish to make Enduring Powers of Attorney, you must both make separate Enduring Powers of Attorney because although a person can appoint several attorneys or make several Enduring Powers of Attorney to run concurrently and several people can appoint the same attorneys, several people cannot make a joint Enduring Power of Attorney.

Although you can create an Enduring Power of Attorney which is limited to come into effect only in specified circumstances, for example after you have become mentally incapable, the Enduring Power of Attorney must be completed while you have the mental capacity to give it and if it is to remain effective after you start to become mentally incapable, it must be registered with the Court of Protection.

To grant an Enduring Power of Attorney you must be able to understand in broad terms the effect of the document and be over the age of 18 and not bankrupt. To be an attorney you must be over the age of 18 and not bankrupt or mentally incapable.

Because the attorney is often given very wide powers the choice of attorney is very important. Your attorney should be a compassionate person who can be trusted to act in your interests. The relevant factors to be borne in mind in the choice of an executor are relevant to the choice of an attorney. (Please refer back to Chapter 4.)

Some solicitors, accountants and trust companies will act as attorneys, but they will wish to charge and you might consider that it is cumbersome and expensive to employ professionals to do tasks that can be done by a layman such as shopping or clearing your home if it is necessary for you to move into residential care. Although your attorney is entitled to out of pocket expenses he can only charge for his service if permitted to do so by the document appointing him.

Your attorney should be willing to accept the appointment and may decline it by notifying you or, if the power has been registered in the Court of Protection, notifying the court. Similarly you can cancel an Enduring Power of Attorney before it is registered with the court or it can be cancelled afterwards if the court agrees. Your death or bankruptcy will revoke the power of attorney as will that of your attorney if he is a sole or joint attorney (as opposed to a joint and several attorney).

If your attorney suspects that you are becoming mentally incapable, his power to act is limited to your maintenance and protecting your assets until the power has been registered at the Court of Protection.

Before registering the Enduring Power of Attorney your attorney must give notice on a special form (EP1 obtainable from the Public Guardianship Office, Archway Tower, 2 Junction Road, London N19 5SZ. Tel: 0845 330 2900 or 0845 330 2963) of his intention to do so to you and to at least three of your closest relatives from the following classes of your relatives specified in priority:

- your spouse
- your children (including any adopted children but not including stepchildren)
- your parents
- your brothers and sisters including half brothers and half sisters
- your child's widow or widower
- your grandchildren
- your nephews and nieces by blood (including children of your half brothers and sisters)
- aunts and uncles related by blood rather than marriage and your first cousins

unless the Court of Protection dispenses with the requirement. This is to allow you and the relatives to challenge the application to register the power, which you and they can do only on very limited grounds. If notice has to be given to any member of a class it must be given to all members of that class.

The application to register the Enduring Power of Attorney is made on form EP2 obtainable from the Customer Services Unit of the Public Guardianship Office and must be submitted to the Office with a fee of £220.00 within ten days of giving notice to the relatives. The fee is chargeable to your assets but if this would cause hardship, the Office has discretion to reduce or waive it.

If it is satisfied with the Enduring Power of Attorney the Office returns the power stamped with its seal evidencing registration and your attorney can then carry on as before. If the power cannot be registered and you are mentally incapable, or you did not make the Enduring Power of Attorney before becoming incapable, an application must be made to the Court of Protection to appoint a Receiver to manage your affairs under the supervision of the court and that is much more complicated and expensive.

PERIODIC REVIEWS, DEEDS OF FAMILY ARRANGEMENT AND TWO-YEAR DISCRETIONARY TRUSTS

Finally do not forget to review your finances and the provisions of your will periodically to check whether your will is still appropriate having regard to changes in

- tax rules;
- tax rates;
- your wealth and the value of your various assets;
- your family and the coming of age of your children;
- your or your beneficiaries' marriages, divorces and the making and ending of friendships.

If your will is not appropriate to your family circumstances and not tax-efficient at the time of your death, it is
sometimes possible for your beneficiaries to change the
will to make it more appropriate to all concerned by
entering into a document called a deed of family
arrangement within two years of your death. If one of
your beneficiaries has died, provided they have the
consent of those who benefit under his will or intestacy,
his personal representatives can also disclaim or vary his
inheritance by entering into such a deed.

If an asset has been redirected once to a different
beneficiary by a deed of variation, it is not permissible
to redirect it a second time, but more than one deed of
variation can be entered into in respect of an estate as
long as they relate to different assets.

Do not rely upon your beneficiaries or their personal
representatives entering into a deed of family arrangement; they may be reluctant to change what they believe to
be your last wishes and it might not be possible to do so.
Any such deed will require the consent of all concerned. If
minors or others without full legal capacity are involved,
an application to a court to approve the arrangement on
their behalf will have to be made and the court will only
give its approval if it considers that the arrangement is to
the minor's benefit. Moreover the court proceedings
might make the time limit impossible to comply with
and court proceedings are expensive.

If the deed is to be effective for tax purposes it must
contain a statement to the effect that the Inheritance Tax
Act 1984 shall apply as if any variation had been made by

you or, as the case may be, any disclaimed benefit had not been conferred by your will. If the effect of the deed is to increase the amount of tax payable a copy of it must be sent to the Inland Revenue within six months of the date of the document.

In the case of any estate where the residue is either partially or wholly exempt from inheritance tax, it would be necessary to carefully consider whether any proposed disclaimer or variation would cause the total value of the non-exempt gifts to exceed the nil rate band as a result of the grossing up rules which are explained in Chapter 4.

Deeds of family arrangement can also be used to vary inheritance rights, which arise on intestacy and in spite of their name need not be by deed as long as they are made in writing.

The formalities for tax effective deeds of family arrangements have to be strictly observed. Such matters require professional assistance and are not cheap. Moreover it is always open to the government of the day to amend the law as to deeds of arrangement. It is much better to review your will regularly and to get and keep it right than to rely upon the possibility of variation after death.

An alternative way of attempting to ensure that your will will be tax efficient and appropriate to your circumstances at the date of your death, whatever changes take place after you make your will, is to create what is known as a two-year discretionary trust by your will, but this involves a great deal of confidence in your trustees and the giving up of some control on your part. To create such a trust you leave your estate to your executors upon trust to divide it as they see fit between certain specified beneficiaries and it is usual to leave a letter with your will to explain to the executors the principles you wish your executors to use in exercising the discretion you have given them. The letter is not binding upon your executors, but if they exercise the discretion and make the division between the three months and two years following your death, inheritance tax in relation to your estate will be calculated as though their decision had been contained in your will. Thus if you use a two-year discretionary trust your trustees will be able to take account of your PETS when deciding how much of your nil rate band remains and how to allocate your estate. You cannot know this when you make your will. Neither can you know for certain when you make your will what the financial position of the individual members of your family will be at the date of your death, or indeed which of your family members or friends will survive you. The two-year discretionary trust can be very useful if you have good executors and you are apt to be tardy in reviewing your will.

Appendix: Specimen Forms and Documents

SPECIMEN FORM OF NOTICE OF SEVERANCE OF JOINT TENANCY

From (*insert your full names and your address*)

To (*insert name(s) and address(es) of other joint owners*)

Re (*insert the address or a description of the property*)

I HEREBY GIVE YOU NOTICE that I (*insert your name and address*) hereby sever the joint tenancy which exists between us in the above property so that in future we shall hold it as beneficial tenants in common AND I REQUEST that you acknowledge that you have received this notice by signing and returning the enclosed copy notice to me.

Dated (*insert date*)

Signed (*insert your signature*)

Note: A notice in these terms should be given to each joint owner. The following should be written or typed as appropriate on each copy notice on the next line following your signature:

'Received a notice of which the above is a copy this   -
day of   two thousand and

SIGNED_____

SPECIMEN NOTE AS TO REASONS WHY A POTENTIAL CLAIMANT UNDER THE INHERITANCE (PROVISION FOR FAMILY AND DEPENDANTS) ACT 1975 HAS BEEN LEFT NO OR ONLY A LIMITED INHERITANCE

To my Executors.

I (*insert your full names*) of (*insert your address*) hereby declare that I have made (*insert 'no' or 'no further' as appropriate*) provision for (*insert relationship, if any, and name of the person concerned*) in my will of this date because (*state reason or reasons, e.g.*

I have made alternative provision for him in my lifetime.

or

I consider that I have fulfilled my obligations to him in my lifetime.

or

I consider that I should devote the majority of my estate to (*insert relationship and name of the person concerned*) whom I consider to be less wealthy and in greater need.

or

I consider that I should devote the majority of my estate to (*insert relationship and name of the person concerned*) who has borne the major part of the responsibility for caring for me in my declining years.

or

(*insert relationship, if any, and name of the person concerned*) has cut himself off from me and I have neither seen or heard from him for (*insert number*) years.

Dated this (*insert date*)

Signed (*insert your signature*).

<u>Note:</u> This document and the will should both be signed and dated with the same date.

BASIC SKELETON FORM OF A WILL WITH THE RESIDUARY BENEFICIARIES TO BENEFIT EQUALLY.

THIS IS THE LAST WILL of me (*insert your full names, address and occupation, if any*)⎯⎯⎯⎯⎯⎯⎯⎯⎯⎯

1.   I REVOKE all wills and testamentary dispositions previously made by me⎯⎯⎯⎯⎯⎯⎯⎯⎯⎯⎯⎯⎯

2.   I APPOINT (*insert full names, addresses and occupations of proposed executors*) to be the executors of this my will, but if neither of them survive me or having survived me both of them shall be unwilling or unable to accept the office of executor or for any other reason the appointment fails to take effect then I APPOINT (*insert full names, addresses and occupations of proposed alternative executors*) to be the executors of my will⎯⎯⎯⎯⎯⎯⎯⎯⎯⎯⎯⎯

3(a)   I APPOINT the person or people who take out the first grant of representation to be obtained in respect of my estate to be the trustees of my estate⎯⎯⎯⎯⎯⎯⎯⎯

(b)   THE expression 'my trustees' wherever used in this my will shall mean the trustees or trustee for the time being whether original, substituted or added⎯⎯⎯⎯⎯⎯⎯⎯

4. I GIVE

(a)   the sum of (*insert the amount in words and in figures*) to (*each of*) the said (*insert the full names of the relevant executor or executors*) absolutely if (s)he shall prove my will

(b)   the sum of (*insert the amount in words and in figures*) to (*insert full names and address of the legatee*)⎯⎯⎯⎯⎯⎯⎯

These legacies are in addition to any other benefit the legatee(s) may receive from my estate⎯⎯⎯⎯⎯⎯⎯⎯⎯

5.   I BEQUEATH

(a)   my (*insert sufficient description of the article given to enable it to be identified and distinguished from any other of your possessions*) to (*insert full names and address of proposed beneficiary*)⎯⎯⎯⎯⎯⎯⎯⎯

(b)   any (*insert sufficient description of the article given to enable it to be identified and distinguished from any other of your possessions*) which I shall own at the date of my death to (*insert full names and address of proposed beneficiary*).

6.   I GIVE DEVISE BEQUEATH AND APPOINT all my estate not otherwise disposed of by my will or by any codicil to my will to my trustees UPON TRUST to use it to pay my debts, funeral and testamentary expenses and the legacies bequeathed by my will or by any codicil to my will and all tax and other fiscal impositions payable on or in respect of my estate or any part thereof as a result of my death and to hold what remains for such of (*insert full names and addresses of the proposed beneficiaries*) as shall be living at the date of my death and if more than one for them for them equally BUT IF any of them shall die before me and shall leave a child or children who survive me such child or children shall inherit and if more than one equally between them the share of my estate which his or her parent would have inherited had he or she survived me_____

7.   I DECLARE that

(a)   no potential beneficiary under this my will shall take any interest thereby unless he she or it shall survive me by one calendar month (*if required insert 'and attain the age of' and a chosen age 'either before or after my death but within twenty one years of my death'*)_____

(b)   when quantifying the entitlement of any beneficiary on my death no account shall be taken of any gifts made by me in my lifetime_____

(c)   my trustees may in their sole discretion and without requiring the consent of any other person appropriate at such valuation as they shall reasonably decide any assets of my estate in or towards the satisfaction of any testamentary bequest made by me_____

(d)   the receipt of the person who seems to my trustees to be the treasurer or other proper officer of any organisation or the parent or guardian of any minor who is a beneficiary under the terms of my will shall be a sufficient discharge to my trustees for the bequest and that my trustees shall not be obliged to check how the bequest is used_____

(e)   unless they have acted with gross negligence or in bad faith in carrying out or delaying the carrying out of or failing to carry out their duties in relation to my will my trustees shall not be held responsible for any losses suffered by the beneficiaries of my estate_____

8.   IF my trustees shall not be aware of the whereabouts of any beneficiary under the terms of my will after having complied with section 27 of the Trustee Act 1925 my trustees may distribute my estate on the basis that such beneficiary has died before me or ceased to exist before my death_____

9.   I EXPRESS the wish that after my death my body shall be buried and not cremated_____

I N   W I T N E S S whereof I have signed this my will the   day of   Two thousand and   _____

SIGNED by the before named
(*insert your full names*) in our   } Testator to sign here
presence and then by us in his

First witness to sign here

and print his name here

and write his address and occupation, if any, here.

Second witness to sign here

and print his name here

and write his address and occupation, if any, here.

Notes

1. It is not necessary to leave a legacy as provided in clause 4(a).

2. The legacies given in clauses 4 and 5 of the above will have been given free of inheritance tax so that any tax payable will be paid out of the remainder of the estate

and borne by the beneficiaries named in clause 6. If it is intended that any of the bequests should bear their own share of inheritance tax insert the words 'subject to inheritance tax' after the description of the relevant bequest and 'except where otherwise stated above' in clause 6 after the words 'as a result of my death'. In deciding whether gifts should bear their proportion of inheritance tax please consider the possible grossing up of gifts discussed in Chapter 4.

3. If clause 4 is omitted from the will the words 'by my will or' should be omitted from clause 6.

4. The words from and including 'BUT IF' to the end of clause 6 should be omitted if it is not intended that children of predeceasing parents should inherit their parents' share.

5. If clause 7(a) is used and the beneficiary's entitlement is made dependent upon reaching a specified age, the words 'within twenty one years of my death' must be included to avoid the risk of the bequest being void as infringing the perpetuity rule.

6. If a beneficiary's entitlement is made dependent upon reaching a specified age consider including the following sub-clause as 7(f)
    'My trustees shall have power in their sole discretion to use for the benefit of any potential beneficiary part or the entirety of the income and capital of my estate to which the beneficiary may become entitled.'

7. If any of the people named in your will are related to you their identity can be further clarified by inserting the relationship.

ALTERNATIVE PROVISION TO BE USED IN THE SKELETON FORM OF A WILL IF YOU WISH TO LEAVE THE ESTATE TO YOUR SPOUSE FOR LIFE OR UNTIL SHE REMARRIES AND AFTERWARDS TO OTHER BENEFICIARIES

Instead of clause 6 insert the following clause:

6.   I GIVE DEVISE BEQUEATH AND APPOINT all my estate not otherwise disposed of by my will or by any codicil to my will to my trustees UPON TRUST to use it to pay my debts funeral and testamentary expenses and the legacies bequeathed by my will or by any codicil and all tax and other fiscal impositions payable in respect of my estate or any part of my estate as a result of my death and to invest what remains and pay the net income produced by the investments to my (*insert husband or wife as appropriate and your spouse's full names*) until (*insert he or she as appropriate*) remarries or dies whichever shall happen first and afterwards to hold the investments and the income they produce for such of (*insert full names and addresses of proposed beneficiaries*) as shall be living at that date and if more than one for them equally BUT IF any of them shall have died before then and shall leave a child or children who are then living such child or children shall inherit and if more than one equally between them the share of my estate which his or her parent would have inherited if he or she not so died.

Notes

1. This clause can be adapted for use if you wish to give a life interest to a beneficiary who is not your spouse but before deciding to leave only a life or other limited interest in your estate, bear in mind what I have written in Chapters 3 and 4 about impoverishing your spouse and about the Inheritance (Provision for Family and Dependants) Act 1975.

2. Do not attempt to leave successive life or other limited interests without taking professional advice or you may well fall foul of the rules against perpetuities.

3. If you decide to leave a life or other limited interest in your estate you should consider including the following additional clauses:

'( )   MY TRUSTEES shall have power to invest the assets of my estate and vary investments in all respects as if they were their own and to borrow upon the security of such assets upon such terms and for such purposes as they think fit_____

( )   MY TRUSTEES shall have power to retain or purchase freehold or leasehold property as an authorised investment and to permit it to be used as a residence for one or more beneficiaries or potential beneficiaries (including life tenants) of the residue of my estate upon such terms as to repair decoration maintenance alterations improvement insurance heating lighting payment of water rates sewage charges and other outgoings as my trustees shall think fit__

( ) THE FOLLOWING statutory provisions shall not apply to my will or to any codicil hereto: sections 11 (1) and 19 of The Trusts of Land and Appointment of Trustees Act 1996_____

( )   MY TRUSTEES shall have power in their sole discretion to use part or the entirety of the income and capital of my estate to which a beneficiary may become entitled for the benefit of the beneficiary_____

( )   I DECLARE that there shall be no apportionment of the income of my estate to the intent that the Apportionment Act 1870 and the equitable rules of apportionment shall be excluded from the administration of my estate_____

( )   UNLESS they have acted with gross negligence or in bad faith in carrying out or delaying or failing to carry out their duties in relation to my will my trustees shall not be held responsible for any losses suffered by the beneficiaries of my estate_____

( )   My trustees may exercise or refrain from exercising the powers contained in my will notwithstanding that in doing so any of them shall benefit personally provided that they act in good faith_____'

4. If you leave a limited interest, such as a life interest, in your estate to your spouse or civil partner it will avoid possible confusion and disputes as to ownership if you also include the following clause:

    'I bequeath my personal chattels as defined by section 55(1)(x) of the Administration of Estates Act 1925 to my (*insert civil partner, wife or husband as appropriate*)'

ALTERNATIVE PROVISION TO BE USED IN THE SKELETON FORM OF A WILL IF YOU WISH THE RESIDUARY BENEFICIARIES TO BENEFIT UNEQUALLY

Instead of clause 6 insert the following clause:

6.   I GIVE DEVISE BEQUEATH AND APPOINT all my estate not otherwise disposed of by my will or by any codicil to my will to my trustees UPON TRUST to use it to pay my debts funeral and testamentary expenses and the legacies given by my will or by any codicil to the will and all tax and other fiscal impositions payable on or in respect of my estate or any part thereof as a result of my death and to divide what remains into (*insert in words rather than figures the relevant number of shares*) shares and to hold (*insert in words rather than figures the relevant number of shares*) shares for (*insert full names and address of the first proposed beneficiary*) and to hold a further (*insert in words rather than figures the relevant number of shares*) shares for (*insert full names and address of the next proposed beneficiary and continue in this way until all the shares have been disposed of*) BUT IF any of them shall die in my lifetime and leave a child or children who

survive me such child or children shall inherit and if more than one equally between them the share of my residuary estate which his or her parent would have inherited if he or she had survived me <u>AND IF</u> any of them shall die in my life-time and leave no child or children who survive me the share given to him or her shall not lapse but shall accrue and be added proportionately to the other share or shares the trusts of which have not failed and shall be held by my trus-tees upon the same trusts as such other share or shares____

Notes

1. If you intended that any of the bequests should bear their own share of inheritance tax insert the words 'subject to inheritance tax' after the description of the relevant bequest and 'except where otherwise stated above' in clause 6 after the words 'as a result of my death'. In deciding whether gifts should bear their proportion of inheritance tax consider the possible grossing up of gifts discussed in Chapter 4.

2. If you do not intend that the children of any proposed beneficiary who dies before you shall inherit the share which the parent would have inherited delete the words from and including 'BUT IF' to the end of the clause and substitute

   '<u>BUT IF</u> any of them shall die in my lifetime the share given to him or her shall not lapse but shall accrue and be added proportionately to the other share or shares the trusts of which have not failed and shall be held by my trustees upon the same trusts as such other share or shares____'

WILL LEAVING THE ENTIRE ESTATE TO SPOUSE AND APPOINTING HER AS THE SOLE EXECUTRIX WITH ALTERNATIVE PROVISIONS SHOULD SHE DIE BEFORE THE TESTATOR

THIS IS THE LAST WILL of me (*insert your full names, address and occupation*)_____

1.   I REVOKE all wills and testamentary dispositions previously made by me_____

2.   IF my (*insert wife or husband and the spouse's full names and address*) shall survive me (*if required insert by one calendar month or other suitable period*) I GIVE DEVISE BEQUEATH AND APPOINT all my estate to my said (*insert wife or husband, as appropriate*) for (*insert her or his as appropriate*) own use and benefit absolutely and APPOINT (*insert her or him, as appropriate*) to be the sole (*insert executrix if you are male or executor if you are female*) of this my will_____

3.   IF clause 2 of my will shall fail the following clauses of my will shall have effect_____

4.   I APPOINT (*insert full names, addresses and occupations of the first proposed alternative executors*) to be the executors of this my will but if neither of them survive me or having survived me they shall both be unwilling or unable to accept the office of executor or for any other reason the appointment fails to take effect then I APPOINT (*insert full names, addresses and occupations of the second proposed alternative executors*) to be the executors of my will_____

5(a)   I APPOINT the person or people who take out the first grant of representation to be obtained in respect of my estate to be the trustees of my estate_____

(b) THE expression 'my trustees' wherever used in this my will shall mean the trustees or trustee for the time being whether original substituted or added_____

<u>6. I APPOINT</u> (*insert full names addresses and occupations of proposed guardians*) to be the guardians of those of my children who are minors at the time of my death_____

<u>7. I GIVE</u>

(a) the sum of (*insert the amount in words and in figures*) to (*each of*) the said (*insert the full names of the relevant executor or executors*) absolutely if (*insert 'he' or 'she' or 'they' as appropriate*) shall prove my will_____

(b) the sum of (*insert the amount in words and in figures*) to (*insert full names and address of the legatee*)_____

These legacies are in addition to any other benefit the legatee(s) may receive from my estate_____

<u>8. I BEQUEATH</u>

(a) my (*insert sufficient description of the article given to enable it to be identified and distinguished from any other of your possessions*) to (*insert full names and address of proposed beneficiary*)_____

(b) any (*insert sufficient description of the article given to enable it to be identified and distinguished from any other of your possessions*) which I shall own at the date of my death to (*insert full names and address of proposed beneficiary*)_

<u>9. I GIVE DEVISE BEQUEATH AND APPOINT</u> all my estate not otherwise disposed of by my will or by any codicil to my will to my trustees <u>UPON TRUST</u> to pay from it my debts funeral and testamentary expenses and legacies bequeathed by my will or by any codicil to my will and all tax and other fiscal impositions payable on or in respect of my estate or any part thereof as a result of my death and to hold what remains for such of my children as shall be living at the date of my death and attain the age of (*insert the chosen age not exceeding 21*) either before or after my death and if more than one equally between them <u>BUT IF</u> any of my children shall not survive me and attain that age and shall leave a child or children who survive me such child or children shall take and if more than one equally between them the share of

my estate which his or her parent would have taken had he or she survived me and attained that age

10. I DECLARE that

(a)   no potential beneficiary under this my will shall take any interest therein unless he she or it shall survive me by one calendar month (*if required insert 'and attain the age of' and a chosen age 'either before or after my death but within twenty one years of my death'*) _____

b)   when quantifying the entitlement of any beneficiary on my death no account shall be taken of any gifts made by me in my lifetime _____

c)   my trustees may in their sole discretion and without requiring the consent of any other person appropriate at such valuation as they shall reasonably decide any assets of my estate in or towards the satisfaction of any testamentary bequest made by me _____

(d)   my trustees shall have power to invest the assets of my estate and vary investments in all respects as if they were their own and to borrow upon the security of such assets upon such terms and for such purposes as they think fit ____

(e)   the receipt of the person who seems to my trustees to be the treasurer or other proper officer of any organisation or the parent or guardian of any minor who is a beneficiary under the terms of my will shall be a sufficient discharge to my trustees for the bequest and that my trustees shall not be obliged to check how the bequest is used _____

(f)   unless they have acted with gross negligence or in bad faith in carrying out or delaying the carrying out of or failing to carry out their duties in relation to my will my trustees shall not be held responsible for any losses suffered by the beneficiaries of my estate _____

(g) the following statutory provisions shall not apply to my will or to any codicil to my will: sections 11 (1) and 19 of the Trusts of Land and Appointment of Trustees Act 1996 ____

11. IF my trustees shall not be aware of the whereabouts of any beneficiary under the terms of this my will after having complied with section 27 of the Trustee Act 1925 my trustees may distribute my estate on the basis that such beneficiary has predeceased me or ceased to exist before my death_____

12. MY TRUSTEES may exercise or refrain from exercising the powers contained in my will notwithstanding that in doing so any of them shall benefit personally provided that they act in good faith_____

13. MY (*insert wife or husband as appropriate*) and I agree that our respective wills are/are not mutual wills and that each of us is/is not free to dispose of his/her property in any way he or she thinks fit in the future_____

14. I EXPRESS the wish that after my death my body shall be buried and not cremated_____

IN WITNESS whereof I have signed this my will this   day of   Two thousand and   _____

SIGNED by the before named   ⎫
(*insert your full names*) in our   ⎬   Testator to sign here
presence and then by us in his   ⎭

First witness to sign here

and print his name here

and write his address and occupation, if any, here

Second witness to sign here

and print his name here

and write his address and occupation, if any, here

Notes to the above will

1. It is not necessary to leave a legacy as provided in clause 7(a).

2. The legacies given in clauses 7 and 8 of the above will have been given free of inheritance tax so that any tax payable will be paid out of the remainder of the estate and borne by the beneficiaries named in clause 9. If it is intended that any of the bequests should bear their own share of inheritance tax insert the words 'subject to inheritance tax' after the description of the relevant bequest and 'except where otherwise stated above' in clause 9 after the words 'as a result of my death'. In deciding whether gifts should bear their proportion of inheritance tax consider the possible grossing up of gifts discussed in Chapter 4.

3. If clause 8 is omitted from the will the words 'by my will or' where they follow 'not otherwise disposed of' should be omitted from clause 9.

4. The words from and including 'BUT IF' to the end of clause 9 should be omitted if it is not intended that children of predeceasing parents should inherit their parents' share.

5. If clause 10(a) is used and the beneficiary's entitlement is made dependent upon reaching a specified age, the words 'but within twenty one years of my death' must be included to avoid the risk of the bequest being void as infringing the perpetuity rule.

6. If a beneficiary's entitlement is made dependent upon reaching a specified age consider including the following sub-clause as 10(h):

    'My trustees shall have power in their sole discretion to use for the benefit of any potential beneficiary part or the entirety of the income and capital of my estate to which the beneficiary may become entitled.'

7. If any of the people named in your will are related to you their identity can be further clarified by inserting the relationship.

ADDITIONAL CLAUSES TO BE INSERTED IN A WILL

In a will made with a marriage in mind

THIS WILL is made with my intended marriage to (*insert intended spouse's full names*) in mind and shall not be revoked by the marriage⎯⎯⎯⎯⎯⎯⎯⎯⎯⎯⎯

IF the marriage takes place the following clauses of my will shall have effect⎯⎯⎯⎯⎯⎯⎯⎯⎯⎯⎯⎯⎯⎯⎯⎯⎯
(*insert the relevant required clauses*)

IF the marriage does not take place the following clauses of my will shall have effect⎯⎯⎯⎯⎯⎯⎯⎯⎯⎯⎯⎯⎯⎯
(*insert the relevant required clauses*)

Note: The above clauses can be adapted for use in a will which is made with a civil partnership in view.

Consider including some or all of the following clauses additionally to those contained in the skeleton will.

In a will containing gifts to under age beneficiaries

Appointment of guardians
I APPOINT (*insert full names, addresses and occupations of proposed guardians*) to be the guardians of those of my children who are minors⎯⎯⎯⎯⎯⎯⎯⎯⎯⎯⎯⎯⎯⎯

Advancement clause
MY TRUSTEES shall have power in their sole discretion to use part or the entirety of the income and capital of my estate to which a beneficiary may become entitled for the benefit of the beneficiary⎯⎯⎯⎯⎯⎯⎯⎯⎯⎯⎯

Receipt clause

THE RECEIPT of the parent or guardian of any minor who is a beneficiary under the terms of my will shall be a sufficient discharge to my trustees for the bequest and my trustees shall not be obliged to see how the bequest is used_____

Power to invest and borrow

MY TRUSTEES shall have power to invest the assets of my estate and vary investments in all respects as if they were their own and to borrow upon the security of the assets and investments upon such terms and for such purposes as they think fit_____

Exclusion of statutory powers relating to trustees' duty to consult with beneficiaries and beneficiaries' power to appoint and remove trustees.

THE FOLLOWING statutory provisions shall not apply to my will or to any codicil to my will: sections 11 (1) and 19 of the Trusts of Land and Appointment of Trustees Act 1996_____

In a will which contains a bequest to an organisation

Receipt clause

THE RECEIPT of the person who seems to my trustees to be the treasurer or other proper officer of any organisation which is a beneficiary under the terms of my will shall be a sufficient discharge to my trustees for the bequest and my trustees shall not be obliged to see how the bequest is used

Bequest and receipt clause for a bequest to a charity

I GIVE the sum of (*insert the amount in words and figures*) to (*insert the correct name of the charity and its registered number*) if it shall still operate for charitable purposes when I die. This legacy shall be used for its general charitable purposes and I declare that the receipt of the person who seems to my trustees to be the treasurer or other proper officer of the charity shall be a sufficient discharge to my trustees for the bequest and that my trustees shall not be obliged to see how the bequest is used.

In a will which contains a gift for life or time-contingent interest

Power of investment
MY TRUSTEES shall have power to invest the assets of my estate and vary investments in all respects as if they were their own and to borrow upon the security of the assets and investments upon such terms and for such purposes as they think fit_____

Exclusion of the rules of apportionment
I DECLARE that there shall be no apportionment of the income of my estate to the intent that the Apportionment Act 1870 and the equitable rules of apportionment shall be excluded from the administration of my estate_____

Advancement clause.
MY TRUSTEES shall have power in their sole discretion to use part or the entirety of the income and capital of my estate to which a beneficiary may become entitled for the benefit of the beneficiary_____

Personal benefit by trustees
MY TRUSTEES may exercise or refrain from exercising the powers contained in my will notwithstanding that in doing so any of them shall benefit personally provided that they act in good faith_____

Exclusion of statutory provisions relating to trustees' duty to consult with beneficiaries and beneficiaries' power to appoint and remove trustees
THE FOLLOWING statutory provisions shall not apply to my will or to any codicil hereto: sections 11 (1) and 19 of the Trusts of Land and Appointment of Trustees Act 1996_____

IN THE WILL OF A TESTATOR INVOLVED IN A BUSINESS.

IF I am involved in any business at the date of my death either as a sole proprietor or partner my executors shall have full power to continue to carry it on either alone or in a partnership or through an agent or agents for the benefit of my estate and they shall be entitled to be indemnified out of my estate for any debts or liabilities reasonably incurred in carrying on the business———————————————————

IN SEVERAL WILLS WHICH CONTAIN RECIPROCAL BEQUESTS.

(*insert name of other party concerned*) and I agree that our respective wills are/are not mutual wills and that each of us is/is not free to dispose of (*insert his/her property or a description of the relevant bequest*) in any way he or she thinks fit in the future.

SPECIMEN FORM OF CODICIL

BY THIS (*insert first, second or as appropriate*) CODICIL

to my last will dated (*insert the date of the will*) I (*insert your full names address and occupation, if any*)————

1.   (*insert clauses to carry out the changes which you wish to make to the will*)——————————————

2.   IN all other respects I CONFIRM my said will————

IN WITNESS whereof I have signed this codicil this   -
day of   Two thousand and   ——————————

SIGNED by the said (*insert your full names*) ⎫
as a (*insert 'first' or 'second' as appropriate*) ⎪
codicil to (*insert 'his' or 'her' as appropriate*) ⎬ Testator to sign
last will in our joint presence and then by ⎪ here
us in (*insert 'his' or 'her' as appropriate*) ⎭

First witness to sign here

and print his name here

and write his address and occupation, if any, here

Second witness to sign here

and print his name here

and write his address and occupation, if any, here

SPECIMEN ATTESTATION CLAUSES FOR USE IN WILLS AND CODICILS IN SPECIAL SITUATIONS

Attestation clause for use in the will or codicil of a testator who cannot write but makes his mark

SIGNED by the said (*insert full names of the testator*) by making his mark in our joint presence after the document had been read over to him and he appeared to approve it and understand it perfectly and then signed by us in his presence

Testator to make his mark here

First witness to sign here

and print his name here

and write his address and occupation, if any, here

Second witness to sign here

and print his name here

and write his address and occupation, if any, here

Note: Instead of the clause in the skeleton will which begins 'I N W I T N E S S' insert the following clause:

IN WITNESS whereof I have set my hand to this my (*insert will or codicil as appropriate*) this day, of Two thousand and _____

ATTESTATION CLAUSE FOR USE IN THE WILL OR CODICIL OF A TESTATOR WHO CANNOT MAKE A MARK OR WRITE

SIGNED by (*insert full names and address of the person signing*) at the request and on behalf of the said (*insert the full names of the testator*) to give effect to this his (*insert will or codicil as appropriate*) after the said (*insert 'will' or 'codicil' here*) had been read over to him and he seemed to understand it perfectly and approve it, the signing and reading over having taken place in the presence of the said (*insert the full names of the testator*) and in the joint presence of the following witnesses who then signed in the joint presence of the said (*insert the full names of the testator*) and the said (*insert the full names of the person who signed on behalf of the testator*) and each other.

(*The person signing to sign his name here*) on behalf of (*and insert the testator's name here*)

First witness to sign here

and print his name here.

and write his address and occupation, if any, here.

Second witness to sign here

and print his name here

and write his address and occupation, if any, here.

Note. Instead of the clause in the skeleton will which begins 'IN WITNESS' insert the following clause:

'IN WITNESS whereof I have caused this my (*insert will or codicil as appropriate*) to be signed this day of Two thousand and _____'

Attestation clause for use in the will of a testator who is blind

SIGNED on behalf of the said (*insert the full names of the testator*) (who is blind) at his request to give effect to this his (*insert will or codicil as appropriate*) by (*insert full names and address of the person signing*) after the (*insert will or codicil as appropriate*) had been read over to (*insert the full names of the testator*) and he seemed to understand and approve the (*insert 'will' or 'codicil' as appropriate*) perfectly the signing and reading over having taken place in the joint presence of the said testator and the following witnesses who then signed in the presence of the said (*insert full names of the person signing*) and of (*insert the full names of the testator*) and each other.

(*The person signing to sign his name here*) on behalf of (*and insert the testator's full names here*).

First witness to sign here

and print his name here

and write his address and occupation, if any, here.

Second witness to sign here

and print his name here

and write his address and occupation, if any, here.

Note. Instead of the clause in the skeleton will which begins 'I N W I T N E S S' insert the following clause:

I N W I T N E S S whereof I have caused this my (*insert will or codicil as appropriate*) to be signed on my behalf this   day of   Two thousand and   _____

SPECIMEN FORM OF LIVING WILL

1. I (*insert your full names, address and occupation, if any*), on the (*insert the date*) make this Living Will and set down as guidance to my family and my medical practitioners these advance directions as to the types of medical treatment I would and would not wish to undergo bearing in mind that in the future I might be unable to express my wishes.

2. IN giving these directions I consider that

- I am in good physical health
- I am mentally competent
- I have considered the matter thoroughly
- I believe myself to be fully informed and
- I do so voluntarily and free from influence by others.

3. IF any of the conditions specified in the first schedule below apply to me and in the opinion of (*insert number*) of medical practitioners I am unlikely to recover a good quality of life THEN I would not wish to undergo any of the treatments specified in the second schedule below but would wish attempts to be made to prolong my life by the treatments specified in the third schedule below if they are appropriate.

The First Schedule referred to above – the conditions.

- I am brain dead.
- I show no signs of cerebral activity.
- I am suffering from permanent mental impairment.
- I have been in a continuous coma for (*insert the number of*) months.
- By reason of mental illness I have been unable to recognise and respond to my family or friends and I have not been aware of my surroundings or able to differentiate between night and day for (*insert the number of*) months.
- I am so disabled that I am completely dependent upon others and my condition is unlikely to improve.
- I am suffering from any degenerative and incurable illness.
- I have suffered (*insert the number*) cardiac arrests.

- I am totally paralysed.
- I am blind, dumb and deaf.
- I am in a persistent vegetative state.

The Second Schedule referred to above – treatment I do not wish to have.

- Attempted resuscitation.
- Artificial feeding.
- Drug therapy.
- Blood transfusions.
- Artificial ventilation.
- Treatment in respect of which the risks are high compared with its likely benefits.

The Third Schedule referred to above – treatment I wish to have if appropriate.

- Artificial feeding.
- Attempted resuscitation.
- Drug therapy.
- Blood transfusions.
- Artificial ventilation.
- Treatment to alleviate pain notwithstanding that it might shorten my life.
- Treatment in respect of which the risks are high compared with its likely benefits.

SIGNED by me (*insert your full names*) in the   Sign your name presence of (*insert full names of the witness*)   here

Witness to sign here

and to print full names and address here.

Note. The conditions and treatments set out in the schedules are specimens only and you will need to amend, omit or add to them to suit your own wishes but any attempt to prevent basic care such as feeding by mouth or washing will be ineffective.

Checklist for Use After You Have Prepared Your Will But Before You Sign It

Have you included or considered the following matters which have been discussed in the preceding text?:

The date the will is made.

Your full names (including any alias or nicknames in which you have property) and your status or occupation and address.

The executor's full names and status or occupation and address.

Have you included a co-executor or an alternative executor and his full names and status or occupation and address in case your first choice dies before you?

Are you contemplating marriage to a particular person in the near future or entering into a registered civil partnership?

Have you set out in your will or in an accompanying letter any burial/cremation/funeral wishes about which you feel strongly?

Have you checked whether any property you own with another person is owned as beneficial joint tenants or tenants in common and remembered that any land or property of which you are a beneficial joint tenant cannot be left in your will and will pass to your co-owner on your death unless you sever the joint tenancy? If there is any jointly owned property in respect of which you are a beneficial joint tenant and which you wish to leave by your will, you should sever the beneficial joint tenancy and create a tenancy in common in your lifetime. You cannot sever it by your will.

Are any pecuniary legacies you have left to bear their share of inheritance tax or is the tax on them to be paid out of the residuary estate?

Are any gifts of specific articles you are leaving to bear their share of inheritance tax or is the tax on them to be paid out of the residuary estate?

What is to happen to the residue of your estate, or the share of the residuary estate as the case might be, if the beneficiary dies before you?

Do you wish to make any of your bequests contingent upon the happening of any event, for example contingent upon survival by a specified period or the attainment of a specified age?

Do you wish your executors to have power, in their discretion, to use money from a bequest or from the income it produces for the benefit of beneficiaries whose gift is contingent upon the happening of any event (for example contingent upon survival by a specified period or the attainment of a specified age) before the event has occurred?

Have you stated who is to be entitled to give your executors a valid receipt and discharge for any gift to a charity or to an under age beneficiary?

If you are a father and were not married to any of your children's mothers at the time of the child's birth, has a parental responsibility agreement been completed and registered or does one need to be registered or completed?

If you are a father and were not married to any of your children's mothers at the time of the child's birth, do you need to have the child's birth re-registered to show you as the father in the registration particulars?

Have you appointed a guardian for any infant children you might leave and in respect of whom you have parental responsibility? Have you made provision in your will for their maintenance from the estate?

In absence of fraud or gross negligence on their part, are your trustees to be relieved from responsibility for any mistakes they might make?

Do you wish to exclude any excludable statutory provisions?

Do you wish your executors to have additional powers to those always given to them by law, for example power to purchase assets from your estate, or to increase their powers to continue any business you have or to advance monies to contingent beneficiaries or the executors' powers of investment?

Do you wish your executors to receive a legacy or payment for the work they do on behalf of the estate? If so, unless they are professional trustees, you must include a clause in the will expressly authorising payment.

Do you wish to include a clause to the effect that legatees shall receive interest on their legacies calculated from the date of your death instead of the usual rule that they are only entitled to interest calculated from the date of death if the legacies are not paid to them within one year of death? Such interest is, of course, paid out of your residuary estate and at the expense of those to whom you have left your residuary estate.

Have you considered any unusual family circumstances you may have, such as a disabled spouse or children and any beneficiaries with special needs?

Have you made sufficient provision in your will to prevent challenges being made to it under the Inheritance (Provision for Family and Dependants) Act 1975 as amended and do you wish to leave a statement indicating why you have made no provision or only limited provision for possible claimants?

Have you considered the effect of any previous marriages, civil partnerships and divorce settlements and whether they exclude any claim against your estate? If they do not, consider whether or not you have made reasonable provision for possible claimants e.g. your ex-spouse, by your will.

Have you made it clear whether any legacies are to be paid in addition to or in substitution for any debts you owe to your beneficiaries?

Have you made a will to deal with any property you own which is not in England or Wales and is that will in accordance with the law of the relevant state in which the property is situated, both as to the formalities for making the will and the substantive law of that country?

Do you need to say in your will in what state you consider yourself to be domiciled?

Is it appropriate to state in the will whether it is a mirror will or mutual will?

Have the trustees of any pension scheme of which you are a member been notified of the way in which you wish them to exercise any discretion they may have in relation to any potential benefits arising from your membership?

If you have, or might have, under age children, have you dealt with guardianship in your will and made provision for maintenance of the children by the guardian?

Have you considered the effect of inheritance tax on your estate? Could your will be made more tax efficient and still carry out your wishes? Have you considered making nil rate band gifts, the needs of your surviving spouse and the assets and income which she has in her own right, whether or not a survivorship clause should be included in the will, what are the needs of the individual beneficiaries and should a generation be skipped?

Have you included in your will everyone you wish to benefit?

Have you considered what is to happen to any pets you might own at your death and included the appropriate provisions in your will?

Glossary

Absolutely – not for the benefit of any other person and free from any condition.

Administrator – the person who winds up the matters left behind after death by a person who does not make a will or who does not appoint anyone who is able and willing to wind them up.

Affidavit –a document the contents of which have been sworn on oath to be true.

Affirm – the word used to mean the making of a solemn declaration by a person who for reasons of conscience declines to swear on oath.

Annulment – making void.

Articles of association – a document which governs how a company is structured and managed including the various classes of the company's share capital and the rights of each class of shares.

Beneficiary – an organisation or person who benefits from or inherits.

Chattels – moveable property.

Civil partner – a person who has entered into the relationship with another person of the same sex which is recognised by the Civil Partnership Act 2004 and registered that relationship in accordance with the terms of the Act which comes into force on 5 December 2005.

Co-executor – an executor who is appointed to act with another executor.

Co-habitees – unmarried people who live together as man and wife.

Codicil – a supplementary document which adds to or amends an existing will.

Contingent – dependent upon the fulfilment of a condition or the happening of an event.

Deceased – dead, the person who has died.

Domicile – the state or country in which you intend to make your permanent home. For a fuller explanation of the meaning of domicile see Chapter 3.

Donee – a person to whom something is given.

Donor – a person who makes a gift.

Estate – the assets which are owned at death.

Executor/executrix – the person appointed by a will or codicil to carry out its provisions after the death of the person who makes it.

Gifts per capita – gifts by which each person takes an equal share as opposed to gifts per stirpes where those who inherit through their parent take equally between them their parent's share and not an equal share with the other members of their parent's class.

Gifts per stirpes – *see* gifts per capita.

Guardian – a person given the powers and responsibilities of the parent in respect of an underage child.

Grant of representation – the document given out by the Probate Registry which gives legal authority to deal with matters relating to someone who has died. The document is a grant of probate if the deceased made a valid will appointing an executor who proves the will or a grant of letters of administration if he did not.

Inheritance tax – the tax payable on a death.

Intestate – not having made a valid will.

Intestacy – the absence of a valid will.

Joint tenants – people who jointly own assets in such a way that by law the ownership passes to the survivor or survivors on the death of one of them.

Legacy – a gift left by a will or by a codicil.

Legatee – a beneficiary to whom a gift is made by a will or a codicil.

Letters of administration – the document issued by the Probate Registry which confirms the right of an administrator (the person appointed by the Probate Registry) to administer the estate of a person who has not made a valid will or who has made a valid will of which there is no executor who is willing and able to act.

Life interest – the right to benefit from something during life but not to dispose of it on death.

Life tenant – a person who has the right to benefit from something during life but not to dispose of it on death.

Minor – a person who is under the age of 18 and who has consequently not reached the age of majority.

Next of kin – the nearest relative.

Nil rate band – the part of an estate the value of which is below the value at which inheritance tax is charged.

Personal representatives – those given authority to represent someone who has died and to administer their affairs – executors or administrators if no executors have been appointed.

Power of appointment – the right to decide who shall have the benefit of an asset or benefit from the income it produces.

Predecease – die before.

Probate – the document issued by the Probate Registry after a death which proves that the will is valid.

Probate Registry – the office of the High Court which deals with matters relating to estates after death.

Residue or residuary estate – that part of an estate which is left after all debts, liabilities and legacies have been discharged.

Revoke – cancel.

Revocation – cancellation.

Spouse – the person to whom you are married.

Tenant in common – someone who owns a share of an asset in such a way the he can deal with it separately from the remainder of the asset.

Testator – a male person who makes a will.

Testatrix – a female person who makes a will.

Trustee – a person who is trusted to carry out or perform a duty or service or hold or manage property for the benefit of another person.

Index

Accumulations
rule against, 115
Active military service, 15
Adopted children
inheritance by, 13
Advance directive, 131–134
competence to make, 133
need to review, 134
requirements for validity of, 133
Alterations in will, 25, 122–123
Anatomy Act 1984, 36
Annulment of marriage, 116
Aunt,
entitlement to Letters of Administration, 8
bequest to, 107

Bank account
bequest of, 109
Bankrupt. *See* beneficiaries
Belongings
meaning of, 111
Beneficiaries
bankrupt, bequests to, 61–63
charitable, 90–91, 99
choice of, 55–65
discretionary trust for, 62–64
elderly, 55–56
protective trust for, 62–63
spendthrift, 61–63
suffering from incapacity, 64–65
young, bequest to, 58–61
Beneficiary
as executor, 43
as witness to will, 113
death of, 90–92
descendant who dies before testator, 91, 115
description of, 106, 107
names of, 106
spouse as, 71, 72, 75–83, 93–95, 116
when conceived but not born, 106
who cannot be found, 99
Bequest. *See* Gift
Body
burial of, 53–54
cremation of, 52, 53
disposal of, 4, 36–37, 51–55
disposal of ashes, 53

use for organ
transplants, 54, 55
use for tissue research,
36–37, 55
when coroner's consent
required for, 37
removal from England
and Wales, 52, 54
Brother, entitlement to
Letters of
Administration, 8
Building Society Account,
bequest of, 109
Burial
at sea, 54
in churchyard or
cemetery, 53
in private land, 53–54
place of to be notified to
registrar, 54
woodland, 53
Business, 14, 29, 32, 45, 56,
72, 100, 112, 162, 170

Charity
bequest to, 90–91, 99,
108
definition of, 90
Charity Commission, 108
Chattles
meaning of, 111–112,
174
Child
meaning of, 8, 107
Children
adopted, 107
appointment of
guardian for, 46–51

bequests to, 50, 86–87,
93–94, 98,
entitlement to Letters of
Administration, 8
illegitimate, 8, 107
meaning of, 8, 107
maintenance of, 50, 51
stepchildren, 107
Civil Partner
claims by under the
Inheritance (Provision
for Family and
Dependants) Act
1975, 38–39, 107
displacement of as
guardian, 5, 50
entitlement to letters of
administration, 8, 9
inheritance rights, 3, 5,
8–13
inheritance tax and, 72,
73, 76–84, 87
parental responsibility
and, 47
shared home and will,
93–95
witnessing will, 22, 113
Civil Partnership
effect of dissoluation of,
116
meaning of, 175
Codicil, 123, 174
Cohabitee
inheritance by, 3
Cohabitees. *See*
Inheritance tax
Creditors
entitlement to Letters of

Administration, 8
Cremation. *See* Body
cremation of

Debts
direction to pay, 96
payable from which
property?, 96
**Deed of family
arrangement,** 141–142
Deed of variation, 141–142
Descendant,
gift to, 91, 107, 115
meaning of, 107
Discretionary trust. *See*
Beneficiaries
discretionary trusts for
Divorce
effect of, 116–117
Domicile 26–27, 118
definition of, 26, 175
of choice, 26
of dependency, 26–27
of origin, 26

Election doctrine of, 34–
35, 110
**Enduring Power of
Attorney,** 134–140
capacity to enter into,
137–138
registration of, 139–140
requirements for, 135
termination of, 139
Entitlement
on intestacy, 8–13
Equity release scheme, 57,
58

Estate
meaning of, 111, 175
Executor
bequest to, 43, 110
exemption from legal
liability, 102
power to buy from
estate, 100
powers derive from, 7
record of information
for, 129–131
right to dispose of body,
4, 37, 51
time executor's powers
arise, 7
Executors
beneficiaries as, 43
choice of, 43–46, 90
co-executors, 42–43
expenses of, 45
fees, 44–46
gift to, 52, 110
information for, 129–
131
mentally ill, 44
minor, 44
number of, 42–43
professional
choice of, 44
remuneration and
fees, 44, 45, 46
Public Trustee as, 46–47

Family
meaning of, 111
Father
displacement of as
guardian, 5

entitlement to Letters of
Administration, 8
meaning of, 13
Finance Act 2004, xv, 69
'From'
meaning of, 83, 112

Gift
choice of assets for, 74–
75
contingent, 58–61
contrary to public
policy, 113–114
description of, 108, 109
effect of reservation of
benefit from on
Inheritance Tax, 68–
71
for national purposes,
72
from income, 71
general charitable
intention, 91
inheritance tax
exemption from
Inheritance Tax, 71–
72
Inheritance Tax,
potentially exempt
from, 67–68
liability for inheritance
tax in respect of, 73,
84
lifetime by the
terminally ill, 76
of matrimonial home, 94
subsequent benefit for

donor from asset
given, 69–71
to aunt, 107
to beneficiary who dies,
90–92
to children, 91, 93
to charity, exemption
from Inheritance Tax,
72
to creditor, 110
to debtor, 110
to descendant, 91, 107,
115
to descendant who dies
before you, 91, 115
to grandchildren, 86–87
to Housing
Associations, 72
to minor, 50, 58–61, 86–
87, 98–99
to non-domiciled
spouse, 71
to survivng spouse, 93,
116
to uncle, 107
to witness or spouse of
witness, 113
valuation for
Inheritance Tax
purposes, 66, 84–86
vesting of, 60–61
void by reason of,
Perpetuity and
Accumulations Act
1964, 106, 115
uncertainty, 104, 108–
109

Goods
  meaning of, 111
Grandchildren
  bequests to, 86–87, 115
  entitlement to Letters of
    Administration, 8
Grandparent
  entitlement to Letters of
    Administration, 8
Guardian
  appointment of 5, 46–49
  by will, 5, 46, 48, 49
  choice of, 5, 51
  executor as, 50–51
  of child of unmarried
    mother, 5, 48
  parental responsibility,
    46–48, 49
  powers and duties of, 46,
    48
  revocation of, 49–50
  Special Guardian, 47
  who can appoint by will,
    47–48
Guardianship
  disclaimer of, 50
  divorce or annulment of
    marriage, effect on,
    116–117
  termination of, 49–50

Home reversionary scheme,
  56
Human Tissues Act 1961,
  36

Immediately Chargeable

Gifts,
  incidence of Inheritance
    Tax on, 73
  meaning of, 67
  rate of Inheritance tax
    on, 66
Income
  apportionment of, 99–
    100
  power to accumulate,
    115
Income tax charge on
  continued use of pre-
  owned assets, 69–71
Informal will
  of person on actual
    military service, 17,
    123
  of seamen at sea, 17, 123
Inheritance (Provision for
  Family and Dependants)
  Act 1975, 38–40, 81, 95,
  107
Inheritance Tax
  action to minimise, 74–
    87
  agricultural relief from,
    72
  basis of charge, 66, 73–
    74
  business property relief,
    72
  calculation of, 66, 73
  cohabitees, 86
  effect of reservation of a
    benefit on, 68–71
  equalisation of estates,

76–78,
exempt gifts, 71–72
extent of liability of non-
    UK domiciled
    persons, 66
foreign property, who
    bears tax on, 96
gifts for national
    purposes, 72
gifts to non-domiciled
    spouse, 71
gifts to registered
    charities, 72
grossing up of bequests
    for purposes of, 73, 84
immediately chargeable
    gifts, 73
definition of, 66–67
incidence of, 73, 96
Inheritance Tax Saving,
    75–87
jointly owned property
liability for Inheritance
    tax on, 73, 84, 96
nil rate band, 67, 77, 78,
    80, 82, 85
on gifts from income, 71
on PETS, 73
potentially exempt
    transfers. *See* PETS
rate of, 66
related property
    meaning of, 85
saving, 75–87
small gifts, 72
statement in deed of
    family arrangement,

141
surviving spouse
    exemption, 71, 86
threshold for payment
    liability, 67
trusts for the vulnerable,
    65
two year discretionary
    trust, 142–143
United Kingdom
    definition of for
        purposes of, 66
UK Domiciled persons
    extent of liability for,
    66
valuation of chargeable
    gifts for the purpose
    of, 66, 84, 85
wedding gifts, 72
who bears, 73, 95–96
**Insurance policies held on
    trust,** 33–34
Intangible assets, 40
International wills, 118–121
Intestacy
    inheritance upon, 1–2,
        8–13
Intestate, meaning of, 1, 7,
    175
Issue
    entitlement to Letters of
        Administration, 8
    meaning of, 8, 107

Joint tenancy
    distinguished from
        tenancy in common,

31
registration of severance of at Land Registry, 32
severance of, 32
Joint tenants. *See* tenancy and jointly owned property
Jointly owned property, 30-32, 73, 84, 96
Joint wills. *See* Will, joint

Legacy. *See* Gift
Letters of Administration,
entitlement to, 8
when required, 7
Life interest
apportionment of income in respect of, 99–100
clauses and notes in respect of, 150–152
payment of outgoings in respect of, 96–97, 151
Lifetime gifts
into discretionary trusts, 67
to companies, 67
Living will. *See* advance directive

Marriage
annulment of effect on will, 116–117
Matrimonial home, 2, 56–58, 94
gift of and inheritance

tax, 56, 70, 94
Minor
bequest to, 50, 86–87, 98–99
power to give valid receipt, 41, 61, 98–99
power to maintain, 98
provision for maintenance of, 50–51
receipts for bequests to, 51
Mirror wills, 28, 29
Money
meaning of, 111
Month
meaning of, 83, 112
Mother
displacement of as guardian, 5, 49
has parental rights, 47
meaning of, 108
Mutual wills, 28–30, 157, 162

Names, 88, 106, 108
Next of kin
meaning of, 107, 111
right to dispose of body, 4, 51
Nominated property. *See* Property, nominated

Organ donations, 54–55

Parental responsibility, 46–48, 49

meaning of, 46–47
who has, 47–48
**Parental responsibility
agreement,** 48
Partner
inheritance by, 3, 6
surviving spouse
exemption, 86
Pension benefits, 41
Perpetuity rule, 106, 115
Personal chattels
meaning of, 111
Personal effects
meaning of, 111
Personal estate
meaning of, 111
**Persons on active military
service**
formalities required for
valid will, 17
revocation of wills by,
123
PETS
incidence of payable
Inheritance Tax 73
meaning of, 67
taper relief on, 67–72
Power
of investment, 98
of maintenance and
advancement, 98
to appoint additional
trustee, 100–101
to borrow, 98
to buy from estate, 100
to appoint new trustees,
100

**Power of appointment of
appointment,** 28, 34, 116
effect of divorce or
annulment of
marriage upon, 116
Principal Probate Registry
address of, 48, 128
Probate Registry
deposit of will with for
safe keeping, 127
Property
immoveable
definition of, 26
immoveable, validity of
will dealing with, 119
jointly owned, *see* jointly
owned property
moveable
definition of, 26
nominated, 35
with restricted
alienability, 35–36
Protective trust, 62–63
statutory form of, 63
Public Guardianship Office,
116–17, 64, 137, 139, 140
Public policy
gifts contrary to, 113–
114
meaning of, 114
Public Trustee, 45–46

Re Figgis, 83
Receipt
for bequest to minor,
98–99
for bequest to

organisations, 98–99
Related property
meaning of, 85
valuation of, 85–86
Relations
meaning of, 107, 111
Residence order, 5, 49
Residuary estate on
intestacy, 10–12
Right to die, 132
Rights of way, 35–36
Roll up mortgage, 57, 58

Seaman at sea
informal will of, 17, 22,
123
revocation of will by,
123
Shares in limited
companies, 36
Signature
confirmation of
testator's, 19–20
each page of will, 25
meaning of, 18–19
on behalf of testator, 19
position in will, 20
witnessing or
acknowledgement of,
19–21
Sister
entitlement to Letters of
Administration, 8
Special Guardian, 47
Spendthrift. *See*
beneficiaries
Spouse

commutation of life
interest on intestacy,
11
death of intestate, 2
entitlement on intestacy,
9–12
entitlement to Letters of
Administration, 8
gift to for life, 93–94
gift to until remarriage,
93–94
meaning of, 13, 86
of witness, bequest to,
113
purchase of matrimonial
home on intestacy, 11
statutory legacy to on
intestacy, 10
survival by fewer than 28
days on intestacy, 9
Statutory will, 16
Surviving spouse
bequests to, 93, 116
Surviving spouse exemption,
cohabitees not included
in, 86
Survivorship clauses,
interpretation of, 83
use of, 81–83

Taper relief, 67-68
Tenancy in common
distinguished from joint
tenancy, 31
Tenants in common. *See*
Jointly owned property
Testamentary capacity

meaning of, 15–17
time required for valid
will, 16
The Anatomy Act 1984, 36–
37
**The Civil Partnership Act
2004,** 3, 46
The Crown,
entitlement to Letters of
Administration, 8
inheritance by on
intestacy, 13
**The Human Tissues Act
1961,** 36–37
**The Inheritance (Provision
for Family and
Dependants) Act 1975,**
38–40, 81, 107
**TheAssisted Dying for the
Terminally Ill Bill,** 132
**The Perpetuities and
Accumulations Act 1964,**
106, 115
The Trustee Act 2000
remuneration of
professional
executors, 44, 45, 46
The Wills Act 1837, 20, 115
Tissue bank, 36–37, 55
Trustees
beneficiary's power to
remove, 101
liability, 102
power to carry on
business, 14, 100
powers of investment, 98
powers of maintenance

and advancement, 98
powers to use funds for
beneficiaries, 50, 59,
98
Trustees of land
beneficiaries power to
remove, 101
duty to consult
beneficiaries, 101–102
Trusts for the vulnerable, 65
**Two year discretionary
trust,** 142–143

Uncle
entitlement to Letters of
Administration, 8

Wedding gifts
inheritance tax, extent of
exemption from, 71
Will
additions after
signature, 25, 122–
123
alterations in. *See*
Alterations in will
amendment of errors in
the preparation of,
122
capacity to make, 15–17
changing after death of
the testator. *See* deed
of family
arrangement
conditional on marriage,
123–124
confirmation of

testator's signature,
19–20
conventions as to
format, 22–24
convention as to names
in, 24
conventions as to
numbering of pages,
22
conventions as to
numbering of
paragraphs, 22
date of, reference to in
codicil, 89, 162
dependent relative
revocation, 125–126
effect of beneficiary or
beneficiary's spouse
as witness to, 21, 113
effect of later will, 125,
126
express revocation, 125
formalities
for international
wills, 118–121
number of witnesses to
testator's signature,
20
requirement for
witnesses to sign will,
20
requirement to be in
writing, 17–18
requirement to be
signed, 18–19
format of date in, 24
in respect of property

outside England and
Wales, 119, 120
joint, 42
living *see* advance
directive
made abroad
requirements for
English or Welsh
recognition of, 118–
121
number of witnessess
required, 20
of blind testator, 19, 25
of illiterate testator, 19,
25
of person lacking
testamentary
capacity, 16, 137
of person on actual
military service, 17,
123
of person unable to
read, 16–17
of person unable to
write, 16–17
position of signature in,
20
power of court to rectify,
104–106
precautions against
fraud, 24–25
proof by copy, 128–129
reasons for making, 1–
15
rectification of, 105–106
required formalities for,
17–21, 118–121

requirements for proof
of if lost or destroyed,
128
requirement of witness
to testator's
signature, 19–20
review of matters
necessitating new will,
140
revocation of, 122–126
revocation of by codicil
or later will, 89, 122
revocation of by
destruction, 124–125
revocation of by
implication, 125
revocation by marriage,
123
revocation by person on
active military service,
123
revocation by
registration of civil
partnership, 123
revocation by seaman at

sea, 123
revocation, dependent
relative revocation,
125–126
revocation, express
revocation of will 125
safekeeping of, 127–128
signature, meaning of,
18–19
signature to, 18–22, 25
signatures to each page,
25
signed on behalf of
testator, 19
what can be left by, 26–
41
Wills
international wills, 118–
121
mirror, see Mirror wills
mutual. *See* Mutual
wills
Writing
meaning of, 17–18